Discovering Weird and Wonderful Places

By

Shelba Oberto

Zion Publishing
Des Moines, IA

Copyright © Shelba Oberto 2013

All rights reserved by International and Pan-American Copyright Conventions. No part of this book may be used in any manner without written permission of the author.

Information found in this book is the most recent factual information available at the time of publication and taken from the attractions' websites, tourism websites, state websites, Wikipedia, personal interviews, and the National Park Services. The characters and their roadtrip are fictitious.

The photographs were either shot by the author, Shelba Oberto and her family, were contributed by the attractions, were taken from tourism websites or Wikipedia, or were purchased from Bigstock photos. In all cases, the source is listed under the photo with the exception of the maps, which were all purchased from Bigstock. The picture of the word, roadtrip, is by iqoncept. The title page sign photo is by juberly, the picture of Jimmy by DenisNata, and the picture of Kaylee by llike. The table of contents map is by Maggie Casanova.

The author espresses deep gratitude to a large group of talented photographers who have made this book possible.

ISBN: 9781492394419

To order copies contact:

Shelba Oberto

(515) 967-5918, (515) 577-2075

obertobooks@gmail.com

Published in the United States of America

Zion Publishing

Des Moines, IA

Dedicated to:

Haley, Nathan, and Cade, the best grandchildren ever.
What fun seeing so many of these places together!

Thanks to:

My husband, Steve, who was supportive during the enormous amount of time I spent researching and writing this book.

My daughter, Dina, who rescued me when my computer skills were inadequate, and her husband, Gene.

Mary Nilsen, my publisher, whose patience, hard work, and expertise have made this book a reality.

Roadtrip
Discovering Weird and Wonderful Places

"Hi! I'm Kaylee, and I'm twelve years old."

"And I'm James, but my friends call me Jimmy. I'm eight years old."

We have lived our whole lives in Maine, but our parents, who are writers, wanted to explore weird and wonderful places in the United States. They hatched a plan: we would travel to every state in the union—all fifty—which meant we were going to have to fly to two of them! So we packed the family camper and said goodbye to everyone at home. Come and join us on this awesome year of adventure, traveling all over the United States!

Skipping a year of school is, of course, out of the question, so our teachers gave us a bazillion lessons to bring along. We do our schoolwork on the road, which is actually fun! Mom, our on-the-road teacher, turns everything into a teachable moment, while Dad, our navigator and camping director, gets us safely from one place to the next.

Along with our regular homework, we are learning all kinds of fascinating things about the places we visit, things we want to share with you.

With the help of the pictures Mom took and others we collected, and the facts we gathered along the way, we are ready to take you with us on our amazing roadtrip.

Kaylee

and

Jimmy

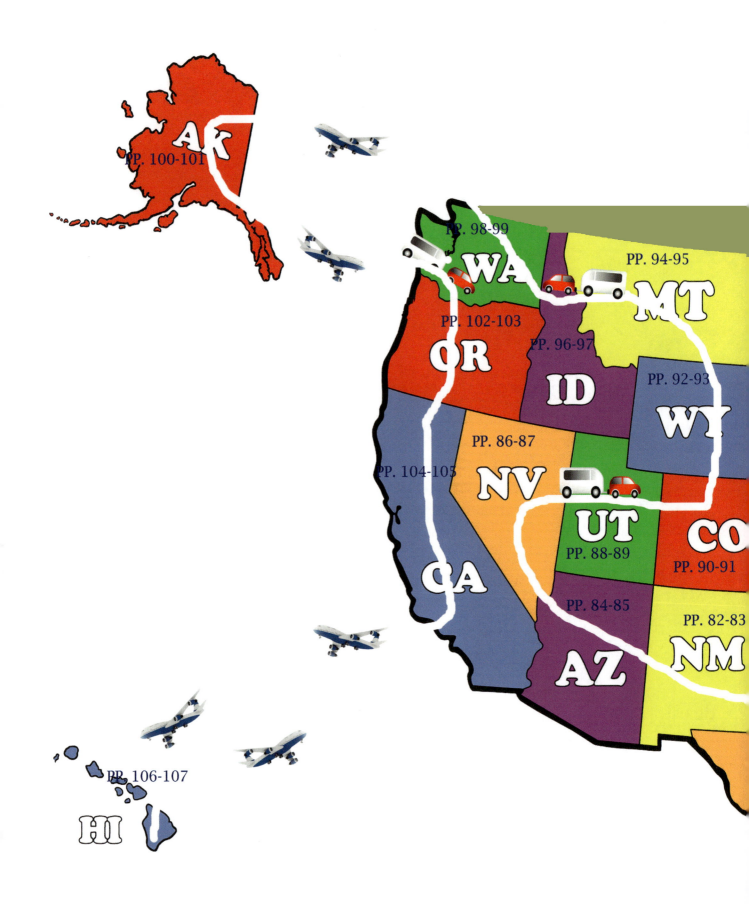

Questions and Activities for each Region on pp. 108-118

NORTHEAST REGION

MAINE

flickr.com/aresauburn

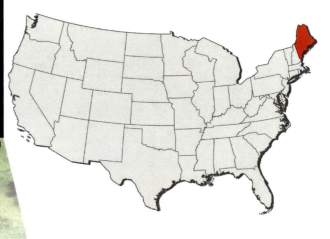

The Pine Tree State

Capital – Augusta

State Bird – Black-capped Chickadee

State Tree – White Pine

State Animal – Moose

Largest City – Portland

Our home state of Maine is a perfect start for our roadtrip across the U.S.! We have vacationed along the rugged coastline and spotted a few of Maine's historic lighthouses. And for years we have feasted on Maine's most famous foods: clams, lobsters, and blueberries. We love the blueberries! We researched our state and found other weird and wonderful places.

Scarborough, ME: "Lenny," a life-size brown chocolate moose, weighs 1,700 pounds and stands in a pond made of blue-tinted white chocolate.

"We bought yummy moose-shaped chocolate suckers!"

Stephen Fazio Photography

Yarmouth, ME: "Eartha," the world's largest rotating glass globe, is housed in a three-story glass building and measures 41 feet wide—the width of a basketball court.

"We found North America and traced our upcoming roadtrip with our eyes."

freeportusa.com

NPS/Todd M. Edgar

Acadia National Park is one of the most visited national parks because of the beautiful rocky coastline and nearby lighthouses.

"We camped near the ocean. It's the Atlantic, you know. At night the sound of the waves crashing into the rocks put me to sleep."

Bass Harbor Head Lighthouse, completed in 1876, still alerts boaters to the rocky coast and invites them into Bass Harbor, all a part of the Acadia National Park. A Coast Guard member and his family live in the lighthouse keeper's cabin.

"Jimmy and I carefully inched our way along the slippery rocks so we could see the lighthouse from the harbor side."

NPS/John Chelko

Little Bay Lobster LLC

Most of the lobsters eaten in the U.S. come from Maine. Brownish orange when caught, they turn red when cooked. But about one in every two million lobsters is blue!

"I haven't seen one in my whole life."

"Do you think the meat is blue also?"

≈ 7 ≈

NEW HAMPSHIRE

Wikimedia Commons/public domain

The Granite State

Capital – Concord

State Bird – Purple Finch

State Tree – White Birch

State Animal – White-tailed Deer

Largest City – Manchester

New Hampshire has it all: mountains and rolling hills covered with trees, lakes, and rivers, and it has 18 miles of rocky coastline. And moose!

"If it's goose and geese, why isn't it moose and meese?"

"Mother said the question created a teachable moment, and now we are doing homework lessons on plurals!"

Bretton Woods, NH: Everyone should do the 2 ½ hour trip on the Mt. Washington Cog Railway, which runs up the highest mountain in the Northeast. The Earth's strongest wind gust of 231 miles per hour has been recorded here.

"That's beyond a hurricane force wind!"

"I didn't know that, but Kaylee actually remembers all the stuff she reads for our homework."

Mt. Washington Cog Railway

Thousands of tourists wend their way through New Hampshire hills in September and October to relish the fall colors. A moose-crossing sign means watch out! There are about 6,000 moose in the state.

"Hitting a moose would not be my idea of fun!"

visitwhitemountains.com

A bull (male) moose weighs between 1,200 and 1,600 pounds and dominates its environment. A moose can have an antler spread of over five feet.

"Hey, that's about as wide as Mom is tall!"

visitwhitemountains.com

Franconia Notch, NH: These unusual tree roots look like octopus arms attacking a huge rock.

"Mom calls them unusual. I call them downright WEIRD!"

NHTourGuide

Franconia Notch, NH: A cool breeze touched our cheeks as we stood on the bridge in Plume Gorge. Scenic waterfalls tumble past the tall, moss-covered, granite walls of the gorge.

"Kaylee grumbled about the two-mile hike."

"I did not! OK, I did, but it was worth it to get here."

visitwhitemountains.com

Jim Teresco

VERMONT

Green Mountain State

Capital – Montpelier

State Bird – Hermit Thrush

State Tree – Sugar Maple

State Animal – Morgan Horse

Largest City – Burlington

Vermont is the only New England state not bordering the Atlantic Ocean.

You cannot go to Vermont without having delicious Ben and Jerry's Ice Cream, which is made here! We highly recommend it!

Montpelier is the smallest state capital in the U.S. (less than 9,000 people). Also, it is the only capital without a McDonald's!

"How can that be possible???"

Richmond, VT: The Old Round Church in Richmond, built in 1812-1813, was constructed as a 16-sided polygon. As legend would have it, the purpose was to not have any right-angle corners where the devil could hide.

"I wonder if it worked."

Louis Borie/Camels Hump Photography

Vermont leads the country in maple syrup production. After the first hard freeze, the trees are tapped using buckets or tubes to collect the sap. It takes 40 gallons of sap to make one gallon of syrup!

"Mom says no more wasting pancake syrup!"

Flariv

Brandon, VT: Standing two stories tall and made of 16 tons of concrete, Queen Connie invites you to sit in one hand while the other balances a full-size golden VW car.

"Who got the crazy idea to build that?"

"Mom saw it as the perfect photo spot."

Fuzzygalore.com

Brookfield, VT: This floating bridge across Sunset Lake is held up by 380 barrels. A replacement bridge under construction will be buoyed up by pontoons instead of barrels.

Central VT Chamber of Commerce/Matt Cyr

"Walking across is funner, anyway. Oops, Kaylee says it should be 'more fun.' Hope Mom didn't hear that, or she'll come up with more homework!"

Troy, VT: Over one hundred covered bridges cross Vermont's streams. The wood in an uncovered bridge will rot in about ten to fifteen years, but by covering it, the bridge will last for centuries. River Road Bridge was built in 1910, over 100 years ago!

"What is it about covered bridges that makes me want to see a lot more of them?"

Wikimedia Commons/Mfwills

MASSACHUSETTS

The Bay State

Capital – Boston

State Bird – Black-capped Chickadee

State Tree – American Elm

State Marine Mammal – Right Whale

Largest City – Boston

Massachusetts is *big* in American history, going all the way back to 1620 when the Pilgrims, in their search for religious freedom, founded Plymouth Colony.

Harvard University, founded in 1636, is the oldest university in the U.S. And in 1647, Massachusetts was the first state to require all towns to have a teacher for the children, laying the groundwork for our system of public school education. This state also played a key role in the American Revolutionary War, as we fought for freedom from England.

Plymouth, MA: The Mayflower II, a full-size replica of the original Mayflower that brought the first pilgrim settlers to the new world, was constructed in England and crossed the Atlantic in 1957.

"It's much smaller than I expected—only 106 feet long and 25 feet wide for 102 people! It must have felt like our camper—cramped!"

"I wanted to *ride* on the Mayflower. But we only got to walk around."

Plymouth, MA: The workers at Plimoth Plantation, a replica of the early settlement at Plymouth, role play the part of Pilgrims. Their names, clothes, accents—everything is like it was back in the 1600s.

"I tried to trip them up with questions about cell phones, TV, and skateboards, but they didn't even know about bathrooms!"

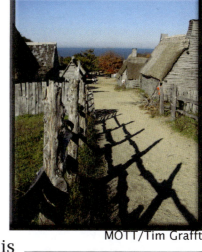
MOTT/Tim Grafft

Boston, MA: Almost hidden among tall apartment buildings is the "Skinny House"—four stories high but only ten feet wide.

"There's barely room to open the door along the side. I wonder how many people live here."

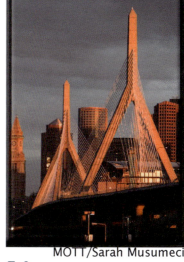
MOTT/Sarah Musumeci

Wikimedia Commons/public domain

Boston, MA: The Zakim Bridge, spanning the Charles River, is one of the widest cable-stayed bridges in the world.

"I'm glad we got to see it lit up at night."

Boston, MA: The 26-mile Boston Marathon, the world's oldest annual race, attracts over 20,000 runners.

"If I start working out now, I could run in it when I'm eighteen. That's ten years to train."

MOTT/Sarah Musumeci

Rockport, MA: The Paper House is made of nothing but layers of newspaper, glue, and varnish.

"It's hard to believe until you see it. Even the furniture is made of newspaper logs."

Brian Beaudry/Tourist Marketing Services

RHODE ISLAND

Rhode Island DOT

The Ocean State

Capital – Providence

State Bird – Red Hen

State Tree – Red Maple

Largest City – Providence

"Rhode Island is so small! Look closely and see if you can find it."

Rhode Island, the last of the 13 colonies to become a state, is only 48 miles long and 37 miles wide. It may be the smallest state, but it still has over one hundred beaches. Playing in the sand, strolling on the beaches, swimming in the ocean—no complaining!

The flying horse carousel in Westerly has 20 horses that are not attached to the floor. They hang from a center frame so they can swing out or "fly."

Once called the Costume Jewelry Capital of the world, Rhode Island is home to about one thousand jewelry-making companies.

Pawtucket, RI: Mr. Potato Heads are made here. Hasbro has made them since 1952.

"I knew Mr. Potato Head was old because Mom says she had one when she was little!"

2009 Hasbro, Inc.

RI Tourism Division

Newport, RI: A lot of water means a lot of boating. Hundreds of yachts sail in the waters along this Atlantic coastline.

"We didn't go sailing, but we did take our first gondola ride!"

RI Tourism Division

Providence, RI: These 36-foot-long, five-foot-wide gondolas hold six people and travel along the rivers that run through the revitalized downtown. Because they are like those in Venice, Italy, Providence claims the name "Little Italy." The gondolier powers the gondola from the back using a 14-foot oar. Thanks, La Gondola!

Wikimedia Commons/Arnold Gatilao

One evening we joined other tourists for a clam bake—a real New England specialty: steamed lobster, clams, mussels, corn…

"I wasn't so sure about the food, but Mom insisted I try everything, and I discovered it's all yummy!"

Providence, RI: Nori, Roof Dragon, the Chinese dragon hanging over the top of the Providence Children's Museum, grabs everyone's attention. But inside—be ready for all kinds of fun!

"Nori's been staring down at people from the top of the museum for over ten years!"

Providence Children's Museum

CONNECTICUT

The Constitution State

Capital – Hartford

State Bird – American Robin

State Tree – White Oak

State Animal – Sperm Whale

Largest City – Bridgeport

"The state song is 'Yankee Doodle.'"

Maine, New Hampshire, Vermont, Massachusetts, Rhode Island, and Connecticut are the six states in the Northeast called New England. We have *tons* of pictures of lighthouses, beaches, museums, and ships.

Connecticut's capital, Hartford, passed the first automobile law in 1901. The law set the speed limit at 12 miles per hour! There were no traffic lights and seat belts were not even imagined yet, so slow was good. The *Hartford Current,* founded in 1764, is the oldest daily newspaper still printing.

New London, CT: Ocean Beach Park draws both tourists and residents of the state with its sandy beach, a water slide, and amusement rides.

"We had a blast on the beach and swimming in the Atlantic! Did you know salt water makes floating easy?"

Dave Sugrue

Dave Sugrue

New London, CT: After trying our hand at building a sand castle, we strolled the beach and admired all the other temporary works of art.

"I wish we could take the credit for this one!"

East Haddam, CT: Gillette Castle, an actual castle with 24 rooms and 47 doors, was built by William Gillette (1853-1937). The weird thing is that no two doors in the castle are alike. Gillette was an actor, director, and playwright who was most famous for his role as the detective, Sherlock Holmes.

raycart

"I kept waiting for a knight to come riding up on horseback. No kidding, the castle was that real!"

jschultes

Hartford, CT: Called the "Father of American Literature," Mark Twain (Samuel Clemens) wrote his classic novels, *The Adventures of Tom Sawyer* and *Huckleberry Finn,* while living in Hartford. His home is now a museum.

"I read Huckleberry Finn *in school last year."*

Mystic, CT: Charles W. Morgan, the only wooden whale ship left in the world, was a U.S. whaling ship for 80 years before becoming a part of this fabulous living history museum town.

"Walking around Mystic Seaport makes me feel like I'm living in an 1800's whaling village."

Mystic Seaport

NEW YORK

Shelba Oberto

The Empire State
  Capital – Albany
    State Bird – Bluebird
    State Tree – Sugar Maple
    State Animal – Beaver
      Largest City – New York City

We need a whole month in New York! Our must-see list is humongous!

In New York City, people are busy going everywhere—on subways (over 700 miles long), in yellow taxicabs (over 10,000 of them), on bicycle and on foot. Never a dull moment!

NPS

Liberty Island, NY: We did it—all 354 steps (22 stories) to the crown of the Statue of Liberty! There are 25 windows and seven spikes (for the seven seas and seven continents).

"We tried to look in every direction, imagining boatloads of people coming to settle in this country."

New York City, NY: The Empire State Building (102 stories) was once considered one of the seven wonders of the modern world. It has recently been remodeled to be more energy efficient. There are 73 elevators that get you to the top in a minute and 6,500 windows.

Michael Slonecker

"I thought of a sign: Window Washers Wanted. Must not be afraid of heights."

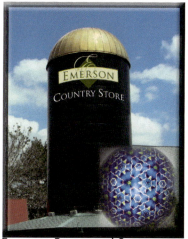
Emerson Resort and Spa

Mt. Tremper, NY: It looks like a silo, but this building holds the world's largest kaleidoscope. The small picture is one of the views in the kaleidoscope—called a mendala image.

"I have a little kaleidoscope at home, but this was so much better!"

Niagara Falls, NY as seen from Niagara Falls, Ontario: Niagara Falls includes three falls: Horseshoe Falls, American Falls, and Bridal Veil Falls. While on the Maid of the Mist boat ride, we were so close to the falls that we *felt* the thunder of the water and the spraying mist. They supply raincoats to keep you dry.

Shelba Oberto. Insets: Dina Parker

"Niagara Falls is lit after dark with colored lights."

NPS/Beth Savage

Flanders, NY: Built by a farmer to sell ducks and duck eggs, the Duck House stands twenty feet tall and has tail-light eyes from a Model T car that cast a strange red glow at night.

"Wouldn't it be fun to live in a duck house and have friends sleep over?"

The World Trade Center Memorial honors the people who worked at the World Trade Center and the firefighters who responded after the terrorist attacks on Sept. 11, 2001. Over 2,800 people died on this devastating day. The impressive One World Trade Center now towers over memorial reflecting pools.

"This gave me goose bumps. I knew about 9/11, but being here made me FEEL it. I wanted to cry.

Dept. of Defense/ Denise Gould   M. Nilsen

NEW JERSEY

NJ Office of Travel and Tourism

The Garden State

Capital – Trenton

State Bird – Easter Goldfinch

State Tree – Red Oak

State Animal – Horse

Largest City – Newark

Of course, no visit to New Jersey is complete without seeing Atlantic City and the famous Boardwalk, which is being rebuilt after the ravages of Hurricane Sandy.

Do you know that Atlantic City is called "Monopoly City"? The Monopoly game board uses Atlantic City street names and places. Monopoly is believed to be the world's best-selling board game.

"Dad always wins in Monopoly!"

Atlantic City CVB

Atlantic City, NJ: Being pushed in a rolling chair on the Boardwalk is the way to go! The popular Atlantic City Boardwalk is the longest boardwalk and was America's first.

"We spent a lot of time swimming in the ocean and rolling around the Boardwalk."

Atlantic City, NJ: The beach patrol monitors the shoreline from a boat.

Atlantic City CVB

"Kaylee thought some of the beach patrol and rolling chair attendants were kind of cute! Now she's mad at me. I wrote this in ink!"

Wikimedia Commons – public domain

Ellis Island, NJ: Half of the American people can trace their ancestors back to the 12 million immigrants who came through Ellis Island between 1892 and 1954. These people, immigrants from other countries, felt both hope and fear as they began a new life here in America.

"Ellis Island gave me goose bumps—GOOD goose bumps—as I thought of my own ancestors who uprooted from their homes and came here so I could have a better life."

Margate City, NJ: Lucy the Elephant is some elephant! She is six stories tall and weighs 90 tons! That is like about 90 cars!

"I climbed the winding staircase in her back leg to get to the howdah (the seat on her back). I could see the ocean from up there."

Atlantic City CVB

NPS

Windsurfing on the breezy Atlantic combines the skills of sailing and surfing. You stand on a wind-powered board that is about three to four meters long and try to steer by moving the sail.

"I wish we could have tried it! It looked like a ton of fun!"

≈ 21 ≈

PENNSYLVANIA

The Keystone State
Capital – Harrisburg
State Bird – Ruffed Grouse
State Tree – Hemlock
State Animal – White-tailed Deer
Largest City – Philadelphia

"Mom is loading us with history lessons because Pennsylvania IS history."

Pennsylvania is the only one of the 13 colonies not on the Atlantic Ocean. To actually be in Valley Forge and Gettysburg and imagine what happened there is, well, there are no words to describe the feeling.

Chocolate lovers, listen up! We stopped in Hershey, Pennsylvania, the "sweetest place on Earth." When Mr. Hershey started his chocolate company, he built a town for his workers!

Philadelphia, PA: The 2,000-pound Liberty Bell tolled loudly in 1776 declaring that the signing of the Declaration of Independence was complete.

"Now that's history!"

Wikimedia Commons/Bev Sykes

Easton, PA: The Crayola Experience has all kinds of activities related to crayons. The world's largest crayon, 15 feet long, 16 inches wide, is here, too. By the way, it's blue.

"There's nothing like getting a new box of crayons. We bought two here, just for fun."

The Crayola FACTORY

Punxsutawney, PA: Punxsutawney Phil, the famous winter-predicting groundhog, lives here. If Phil sees his shadow on February 2, he returns to his hole, and we are doomed to six more weeks of winter.

"What I didn't know is that Phil has a 'wife' named Phyllis!"

Wikimedia Commons/Aaron Silvers

Hellam, PA: The owner of Haines Shoe Company built the Shoe House for guests who came to do business at the company. The guests had a cook, maid, and chauffeur. We toured the five levels of the house.

"Then we had GOOD ice cream."

Linda Mack

Langhorne, PA: Sesame Place, the only theme park in the U.S. based on SESAME STREET characters, has more fun activities and rides than we had time for.

"Jimmy begged to blast off on Elmo's UFO, but then screamed when they shot into the air!"

Sesame Place

DELAWARE

Del DOT/James Pernol

The First State

Capital – Dover

State Bird – Blue Hen

State Tree – American Holly

State Animal – Grey Fox

Largest City – Wilmington

Delaware became the first state to approve the U.S. Constitution in 1787. Delaware has a state star—the Delaware Diamond, and a state dessert—peach pie.

NASCAR fans flock to Delaware, home of the Dover International Speedway. Nicknamed "The Monster Mile," it was built in 1969 and holds 135,000 screaming fans. We saw a monster there. No kidding—keep reading and check out the picture!

Dolores Michels

Dover, DE: The Monster Monument is about as tall as eight 6-foot men standing on top of each other. The Monster holds a *FULL-SIZED* stock car in his right hand as if he is going to throw it at you!

"Did you get that? It's a FULL-SIZED car!"

Dover, DE: High above the "Monster Mile" track, the Monster Bridge allows fans to look down on the speeding cars. No other seats in sports put fans so close to the action!

"Awesome! We were right over the cars."

DE Tourism

Wilmington, DE: This replica of the Kalmar Nyckel pays tribute to a ship that brought people to North America from Finland and Sweden. In the 1600s, the original ship made four round-trip Atlantic crossings—more than any other ship at that time. It holds about 50 passengers and 24 crew members.

Mike Baker

"The cat, Toolbox, who is the star of two books, just retired from her 'work' on the ship."

New Castle, DE: The books in the Old Library, built in 1892, were available only to members until 1942, when it became a public library. This Victorian brick building, now a museum, has six sides.

"A five-sided building is a pentagon, and a six-sided building is a hexagon."

New Castle Historical Society

Winterthur, DE: The Enchanted Woods garden is like something in a fairy tale. This is the Tulip Tree House.

A. E. Crane – public domain

"I would have loved this in our back yard when I was little."

The stone Faerie Cottage is another house in the Enchanted Woods.

"I like the Faerie Cottage best."

Wikimedia Commons/Gregory Kohs

MARYLAND

Wikimedia Commons – public domain

The Old Line State

Capital – Annapolis

State Bird – Baltimore Oriole

State Tree – White Oak

State Reptile – Terrapin

Largest City – Baltimore

"Hello from Maryland! The state sport here is jousting."

The Chesapeake Bay, a great estuary, divides the state of Maryland into two parts. An estuary is a special ecosystem or environment where fresh river water mixes with salty ocean water.

"The Star-Spangled Banner" was written in Maryland. Francis Scott Key wrote the words during the War of 1812 as the British attacked Fort McHenry.

Rock State Park, MD: We love rock climbing. Rock State Park has climbs for just about everyone—from 8 feet to 115 feet.

"We need more practice before we try anything like these guys!"

"But at least Dad let us try climbing on the shorter rocks."

Maryland Office of Tourism

Don Rejonis

Germantown, MD: "Earthoid," the Mother Earth water tower painted to look like the earth from space, measures 100 feet wide and holds two million gallons of water. Sometimes called "The Big Blue Marble," this awesome paint project took a five-person team three months to finish! It was recently repainted, but they kept the earth design.

"I would love to see the earth from space someday."

Assateague Island, MD: If you love horses and beaches, this is a winning combination! Over 300 beautiful wild horses roam freely on Assateague Island and nearby Chincoteague Island, Virginia. The book, *Misty of Chincoteague*, also made into a movie, is a true story about a brother and sister and a real pony named Misty.

Maryland Office of Tourism

"People and horses sharing a beach—so cool if you're careful where you step."

Maryland Office of Tourism

Annapolis, MD: We missed the U.S. Naval Academy graduation, but this picture shows the tradition of Midshipmen throwing their caps in the air.

"Looks like fun, but how do they get their caps back?"

Wikimedia Commons/Derek Ramsey

Havre de Grace, MD: Concord Point Lighthouse and Keeper's Dwelling is the oldest continuously-operated lighthouse in Maryland. It was decommissioned in 1975, and now the light keeps glowing with the help of volunteers.

≈ 27 ≈

WASHINGTON, DC
THE CAPITAL OF THE UNITED STATES

Wikimedia Commons/Everaldo Coelho

Washington, DC (District of Columbia) has all three branches of the federal government: Congress, the President, and the Supreme Court. Beautiful national monuments fill the area on or near the expanse of land called the National Mall. And museums! We could spend a week at the Smithsonian alone!

The Washington Monument: This obelisk—a tall, thin, four-sided, tapering building with a pyramid at the top—is about as tall as a 55-story building (555 feet). That makes it the tallest structure in Washington, DC and the world's tallest stone structure.

"Flags from all the states are around the outside. We found the flags for the states we have visited."

byways.org/Amy Davis – public domain

The Lincoln Memorial at the west end of the National Mall honors Abraham Lincoln who served during the Civil War as our 16th president. Martin Luther King, Jr. made his "I Have a Dream" speech on the steps of the Lincoln Memorial in 1963.

The statue of Lincoln sitting down inside the memorial is 19 feet tall. The memorial has about six million visitors a year.

"Jimmy stood forever looking at the statue of Lincoln. He's really into this history thing now!"

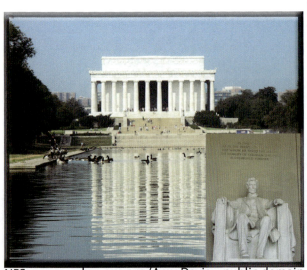
NPS   byways.org/Amy Davis – public domain

Eric Long/Smithsonian Institution

From the north side of the White House, you can see two of the six levels. Within, 132 rooms (over 30 bathrooms!) house five full-time chefs, a swimming pool, a theater, a bowling lane, a tennis court, a basketball court, jogging track, and more....

"Just think! The President of the United States and the First Family live here. I wish we could have seen them."

The White House seems bigger when viewed from the south side. The west wing provides space for the President's office (Oval Office) and many other offices. The First Lady's office is in the east wing.

"Marine One, the presidential helicopter, takes off and lands on the South Lawn."

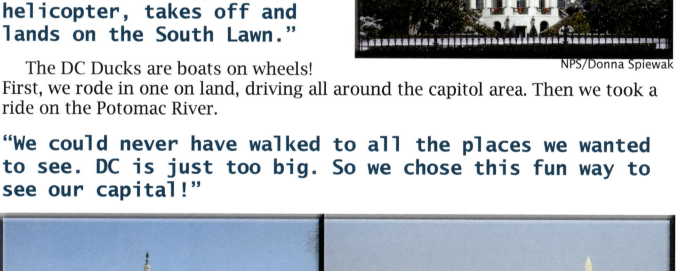
NPS/Donna Spiewak

The DC Ducks are boats on wheels! First, we rode in one on land, driving all around the capitol area. Then we took a ride on the Potomac River.

"We could never have walked to all the places we wanted to see. DC is just too big. So we chose this fun way to see our capital!"

Historic Tours of America, Inc   Historic Tours of America, Inc

SOUTHEAST REGION
VIRGINIA

- The Old Dominion
- Capital – Richmond
- State Bird – Cardinal
- State Tree – Dogwood
- State Dog – American Fox Hound
- Largest City – Virginia Beach

Jamestown, founded in 1607, was the first permanent English settlement in North America. Unfortunately, slavery was introduced there in 1619.

Eight U.S. presidents were born in Virginia, making this state the "Mother of Presidents."

Two of Virginia's historic homes are George Washington's Mount Vernon and Thomas Jefferson's Monticello.

Virginia Beach, VA: Standing four stories tall, Hugh Mongous welcomed us to Ocean Breeze Waterpark, where we tried 6 of the 16 waterslides and swam in a one-million-gallon wave pool.

"I have one word—F-U-N!"

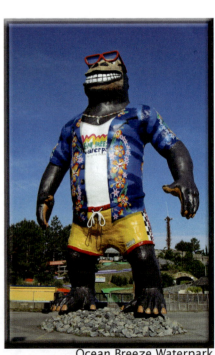

Ocean Breeze Waterpark

Williamsburg, VA: While standing in Presidents Park, an outdoor museum, we were surrounded by presidents. Actually, they are 16- to 18-foot cement busts of all the presidents. President Obama is the forty-third.

"Now I can say I've seen all the presidents."

Presidents Park

Wikimedia Commons – public domain

Natural Bridge: We felt like tiny toy people standing under this twenty-story high natural bridge.

"I wonder if you could even see us from the top or would we look like ants?"

Purcellville, VA: The figure of Christ is cut out of this three-story tall steel cross. A light from behind gives the impression of Jesus floating in the air. The artist created it as an icon of hope.

Tomas J. Fernandez

Arlington, VA: Cape Charles Lighthouse? No. A water tower.

"Not much help in a fog, but great if you need a bath!"

The Pentagon is the headquarters for the U.S. military and one of the world's largest office buildings. About 23,000 people work here. The building has five sides, five floors above ground (and two basement levels), five ring corridors or hallways on each floor, making 17.5 miles of corridors, and 100,000 miles of telephone cables!

Bryan Lambert/citydata

"We were able to join a tour and walk a few of those miles of corridors. The place is huge!"

freephotovault – public domain

WEST VIRGINIA

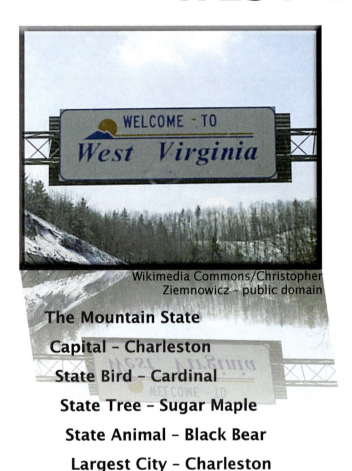
Wikimedia Commons/Christopher Ziemnowicz – public domain

The Mountain State

Capital – Charleston

State Bird – Cardinal

State Tree – Sugar Maple

State Animal – Black Bear

Largest City – Charleston

Three-fourths of the state is covered by forests. That is a lot of trees. The state is said to be the northern-most southern state and the southern-most northern state.

"Huh?"

Fayetteville, WV: New River Gorge Bridge fact list—

* The longest, single steel arch bridge in the U.S. (more than a half mile).

* 876 feet high (higher than two Statues of Liberty with the Washington Monument on top).

* Bridge is closed to traffic every October on Bridge Day so people can parachute or rappel (bungee jump) off the bridge.

* About 80,000 people come to watch hundreds of jumpers.

"Huge event! Not sure I could jump but would like to watch."

Southern WV CVB

flickr/Jimmy Emerson

Chester, WV: We just saw the world's largest teapot. Built to promote the area's teapot industry, it stands 14 feet tall and measures 14 feet wide.

"Do you know the song, 'I'm a little teapot, short and stout'?"

Berkeley Springs, WV: Sadly, the Berkeley Springs Castle, with its 13 rooms, is closed to the public (that means us). So this created a great homework idea—research information about castles: knights, armor, moats, shields, swords, jousting… everything we could ever want to know!

"We've decided we want to live here. Especially since we're getting VERY tired of the camper!"

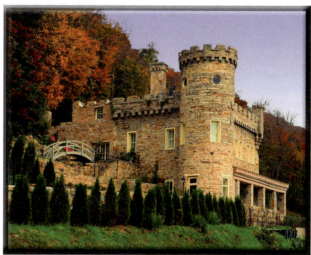
Travel Berkeley Springs/Steve Shaluta – public domain

Southern WV CVB

The Allegheny Mountains of West Virginia, with their curvy roads going up and down, are part of the Appalachian Mountain chain. Unlike the mountains we will see in the western U.S., these mountains are lower and covered with trees.

"I feel like I'm floating in an ocean of trees."

KENTUCKY

The Bluegrass State
Capital – Frankfort
State Bird – Cardinal
State Tree – Tulip Poplar
State Wild Animal – Gray Squirrel
Largest City – Louisville

The U.S. has a lot of gold! Actually, over $6 billion worth is stored in underground vaults. The largest amount of gold stored anywhere in the U.S. is at Fort Knox, Kentucky, about 35 miles from Louisville. No visitors are allowed!

Louisville, KY: The famous Kentucky Derby, for three-year-old thoroughbred horses, is held annually at Churchill Downs after a two-week festival.

Neal Cousland

"I wish we could have seen a race. I love horses."

Mammoth Cave National Park, KY: Silence hangs in the air until someone moves or speaks. Then the sound is loud and echoes throughout the cave. The Introduction to Caving Tour gives families information so they can explore together.

"We had homework about spelunking (cave exploring)."

NPS

NPS

Mammoth Cave National Park, the longest cave system in the world, has underground passages that go on for more than 390 miles.

"We didn't go in quite that far. But I can't wait to tell the kids back home that I'm a spelunker!"

NPS
NPS

Big South Fork National River and Recreation Area: Chimney Rock (20 feet tall) and Needle Arch are examples of some *weird* erosion. The sandstone was carved by wind and water.

Wikipedia/Mason Brock – public domain

"Mom turned this into a science field trip, telling us all about how wind and water carve stone."

Whitley City, KY: Reaching Yahoo Falls was a one-mile hike. We even walked behind the waterfall. This is Kentucky's highest waterfall (113 feet). See the man in the picture? Look just above the log at the bottom of the falls.

"Now I've seen the back side of water! Get it?"

Louisville, KY: Here, the Slugger Museum and Factory demonstrates how millions of baseball bats are made every year. On the side of the building stands the world's largest bat—120 feet tall, nine feet wide at the base, weighing 68,000 pounds, made of steel, and hand-painted to look exactly like a Louisville Slugger.

"68,000 pounds! That's more than the weight of six male elephants!"

Louisville Slugger Museum and Factory

TENNESSEE

The Volunteer State
Capital – Nashville
State Bird – Mockingbird
State Tree – Tulip Poplar
State Animal – Raccoon
Largest City – Memphis

Country music fans know that Nashville is the country music capital of the world. The Grand Ole Opry has the longest running live radio program in history.

The worst earthquake in American history was in Missouri but also affected part of Tennessee. Reelfoot Lake was made by the New Madrid earthquakes of 1811-1812.

Crossville, TN: The book and movie, *Swiss Family Robinson*, is about a family that lived in a tree house. But theirs was nothing like the Minister's Tree House, which is ten stories tall! Horace Burgess says God gave him a vision, and he spent 17 years building this tree house around an 80-foot-tall, 12-foot-wide oak tree. Six other trees help add support.

"I wasn't expecting a tree house this big! I wanted to stay overnight. Unfortunately it was closed."

Sparky Photography

Chattanooga, TN: The Space House on Signal Mountain even has a drop-down airplane door.

"Space House is out of this world! Get it? Space...out of this world...

"My buddies back home would love this!"

Chattanooga, TN: Ruby Falls on Lookout Mountain has a 145-foot waterfall deep *underground*. Above ground is the world's steepest passenger railway.

Sweetwater, TN: Lost Sea is America's largest *underground* lake.

"If you don't mind being underground, Ruby Falls and the Lost Sea boat ride are both a lot of fun."

Ruby Falls

Lost Sea

Memphis, TN: Graceland Mansion was the home of Elvis Presley (1935–1977), King of Rock 'n' Roll. His music was so popular that he became known as just "The King." Graceland is the second most visited home in America. The most visited? The White House.

Wikimedia Commons/Martin Haase

"Mom's SO EXCITED! She loved Elvis Presley! We've been listening to his music for hours in the car."

NPS

Great Smoky Mountains National Park: It takes no time for travelers to discover why this park is the most visited national park in the U.S.

"We stopped in Pigeon Forge and then roamed through the park. Photos can't capture the calm beauty of the place!"

NORTH CAROLINA

The Tar Heel State
Capital – Raleigh
State Bird – Cardinal
State Tree – Pine
State Animal – Gray Squirrel
Largest City – Charlotte

Atlantic Ocean to the east, Blue Ridge Mountains on the west. You cannot beat that!

Virginia Dare, the first English child born in America, was born in North Carolina in 1587.

The first Pepsi was made and served here in 1898.

"Krispy Kreme donuts started in Winston-Salem!"

Hatteras Island: Cape Hatteras is America's tallest lighthouse (208 feet). That is about like 34 six-foot men stacked on top of each other. Because of erosion, the 4,830 *ton* lighthouse was lifted and moved back from the ocean about a half mile in 1999.

"Jimmy couldn't believe it had been moved, but it's true. I did my homework!"

Chimney Rock at Chimney Rock State Park

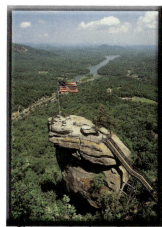
Chimney Rock at Chimney Rock State Park

Chimney Rock State Park: These rock climbers are better than we are!

We went to the top of Chimney Rock (26 stories). It takes 20 minutes walking or 30 seconds by elevator.

"Guess which we did?"

Wikimedia Commons/JcPollock

Asheville, NC: Biltmore House is fantastic! Its 250 rooms make it the largest house in the U.S. There are 65 fireplaces, 35 bedrooms, a library with 10,000 books, a bowling alley, an indoor pool, and an 8,000 acre backyard.

"AND there are 43 bathrooms. That's very important!"

NPS

Kitty Hawk, NC: The Wright Brothers National Monument marks where Orville and Wilbur Wright took their first flight in 1903. The U.S. Navy Blue Angels are doing a flyover in this picture. Cool!

"Since I like airplanes, I did homework about Kitty Hawk before we came. That makes Mom happy."

This photo of driving the Blue Ridge Parkway Linn Cove Viaduct through the Appalachian landscape gave us a glimpse of the beauty of these mountains in the fall.

Daveallenphoto

SOUTH CAROLINA

The Palmetto State
Capital – Columbia
State Bird – Carolina Wren
State Tree – Palmetto
State Animal – White-tailed Deer
Largest City – Columbia

We saw Charleston, South Carolina, by carriage which seemed appropriate as our horses trotted through neighborhoods with classic old homes and beautiful gardens.

The Civil War was a devastating time in our country's history. The nation was divided over slavery. Some states separated from the United States and became the Confederate States of America. Confederates fired their cannons upon Fort Sumter, South Carolina, in 1861. The Civil War began.

Columbia, SC: Eddie, here at the EdVenture Children's Museum, is the world's largest kid (plastic, not real). He is 40 feet tall sitting down. You can climb his vertebrae up to his brain, crawl through his heart, bounce around in his stomach, and slide through his intestines, all the while learning how our bodies work.

"A body tour! Wish I could move Eddie to Maine. This would be a great class field trip."

EdVenture Children's Museum

Charleston, SC: Alabaster is an albino alligator (white with pink eyes) that lives at the South Carolina Aquarium. There are fewer than 50 living albino alligators. Alabaster is almost seven feet long and weighs over 100 pounds. Because albinos are sensitive to light, they cannot live in the wild.

SC Aquarium

"Jimmy wanted to text his friends about the 'swamp ghost.'"

SC Dept. of Parks, Recreation and Tourism

Wikipedia Commons/ Moody Grove

Loggerhead turtles are an endangered species, so sometimes park rangers and volunteers relocate the nests for protection, uncover hatched eggs, and record the number of hatched eggs, undeveloped eggs, and dead hatchlings. Hatchlings unable to climb to the surface are helped to begin their journey to the sea.

"They hatch at night and then the tiny turtles head for the ocean."

Myrtle Beach CVB

Myrtle Beach, SC: The Family Kingdom Water Park, the only seaside amusement park and water park along this stretch of beach, is wet and wild. One slide has a 100-foot drop!

"Wet and wild? No kidding!"

Myrtle Beach claims the title of "miniature golf capital of the world."

"There are a million mini-golf courses! Well, actually, there are about fifty."

Myrtle Beach CVB

GEORGIA

Tracy Quinton

Empire State of the South
Capital – Atlanta
State Bird – Brown Thrasher
State Tree – Live Oak
State Animal – Right Whale
Largest City – Atlanta

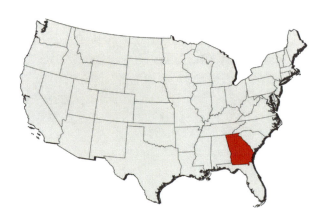

Georgia grows a lot of peanuts, pecans, and peaches. It is often called "The Peach State."

Coca-Cola was first made in Atlanta in 1886 and sold for five cents a glass.

Much of Atlanta was burned during the Civil War. Now many people visit the birthplace and burial site of Martin Luther King, Jr., the Civil Rights Movement leader who said, "I Have a Dream."

President Franklin Roosevelt, who suffered from polio, built The Little White House in Warm Springs, so he could use their mineral springs.

Cleveland, GA: We never knew there were hospitals for dolls, but Babyland General Hospital is the birthplace of the Cabbage Patch Kids. Then they wait for caring families to adopt them.

"Mom had a Cabbage Patch Kid when she was a girl, and now I have one!"

Original Appalachian Artworks

Atlanta, GA: The Georgia Aquarium is the world's largest aquarium with over eight million gallons of water! The outside looks like a huge ship. They have whale sharks and mantas which are the largest of all the rays.

Georgia Aquarium

"I was eye to eye with two manta rays! Scary, even though I knew there was glass between us. I wanted to sleep there, with the fish swimming over me, but Mom said we had to sleep in the camper."

Stone Mountain Park

Atlanta, GA: A cable car at Stone Mountain Park took us up 825 feet to see the Confederate Memorial Carving. Three Civil War heroes on horseback are carved into the granite rock.

"The carving is larger than a football field."

Gaffney, GA: The Peachoid is a four-story water tower that looks like a *giant peach*! Fifty gallons of paint were combined to make over twenty colors for the tower.

Wikimedia Commons – public domain

Carter Center

Plains, GA: President Jimmy Carter, our 39th president, grew up on a peanut farm outside of Plains.

Plains, GA: The 13-foot "smiling peanut" honors both the Carter smile and the state crop.

"I had this crazy dream last night about water towers that looked like peanuts and smiling peaches."

flickriver

FLORIDA

Dina Parker

Florida means Walt Disney World and Mickey Mouse! But there are scads of other things to see in Florida—Everglades National Park, Epcot, Kennedy Space Center, Daytona International Speedway, St. Augustine (the oldest city in the U.S., founded in 1585)—to name a few!

"We all love Mickey Mouse! But we discovered much more to love in Florida."

The Sunshine State
Capital - Tallahassee
State Bird - Mockingbird
State Tree - Sabal Palm
State Animal - Manatee
Largest City - Jacksonville

Near Orlando, FL: The Kennedy Space Center tour fascinated us. It is unusual to see space shuttles on both launch pads! Atlantis is in front, and Endeavour is in the back.

NASA/Troy Cryder

This picture shows an early evening Endeavour launch. We have to pretend we were there. We REALLY hoped to see a liftoff, but that did not happen!

"Science is my favorite subject so they had to drag me out of the space center. That was after I talked them into buying me an astronaut suit."

NASA/Tony Gray, Tom Farrar

North America's only living coral reef is being damaged by divers and boats. A colony grows between a half inch and seven inches a year depending upon the species.

"People! We need to take better care of our planet!"

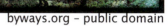
byways.org – public domain

Merritt Island, FL: This American alligator is at the Merritt Island National Wildlife Reserve near Kennedy Space Center. No longer endangered, they have actually become a nuisance in some parts of Florida.

"Kaylee says nuisance means pest. Don't look at me!"

Mary Beth Seibert – public domain

Orlando, FL: With the help of a little mouse, Walt Disney World became the most visited theme park. We love Mickey, Minnie, Goofy, Pluto... all of them! Cinderella's Castle is where Tinker Bell takes her 15 miles-per-hour, 34-second flight each night to Tomorrowland.

The "Earful" Tower has no water in it, but it is part of Walt Disney World's magic.

Dina Parker

"I love WDW...the parades (especially the electrical parade), the characters, the fireworks, everything! I don't want to leave, but we're heading for Alabama in the morning."

Wikimedia Commons – public domain

ALABAMA

The Heart of Dixie
Capital – Montgomery
State Bird – Yellowhammer
State Tree – Longleaf Pine
State Animal – Black Bear
Largest City – Birmingham

Alabama: Think cotton, Helen Keller, Civil Rights Movement, sea turtles. In 1955 in Montgomery, Alabama, Rosa Parks refused to give up her seat on the bus to a white person. Her action sparked action and reaction all over the country. She is now known as the "mother of the Civil Rights Movement."

"I love hearing stories about the Civil Rights Movement."

Crane Hill, AL: Guests at the Anchorlight Bed and Breakfast get a ride on Maggie, the tugboat. Captain Jon and his wife, also Maggie, treat you like family.

"Sleeping in a lighthouse! Awesome! Didn't even miss the camper. Ha! And the food was great!"

Anchorlight Bed and Breakfast

Wikimedia Commons/Andre Natta

Birmingham, AL: The Vulcan Statue, the world's largest cast iron statue, is the symbol of this city. Fifty-six feet from toe to spear point, it stands atop a pedestal that is about 13 stories tall.

Tuscumbia, AL: Since Helen Keller is studied in school, visiting her home was like a field trip. She could not hear OR see! This picture shows actresses playing the parts of Helen and her teacher, Anne Sullivan. This scene from a Helen Keller movie shows Miss Sullivan spelling W-A-T-E-R into Helen's hand, which led to her understanding the connection between things and their names.

Janice M. Williams, Colbert County Tourism

"And we complain? Imagine not seeing or hearing!"

Rob Balmut

Gulf Coast: Between May and October, these popular Alabama beaches are shared with momma sea turtles looking for safe nesting places.

`"The hatchlings seem too small to crawl off into a huge ocean."`

Huntsville, AL: At the U.S. Space and Rocket Center, the world's largest museum about space, we learned about their Space Camp program, which teaches kids about space exploration. Also at the terrific Rocket Park, we saw a model of the Saturn V rocket that took astronauts to the moon.

"Pathfinder, a full-size space shuttle model, closely resembles an actual shuttle orbiter."

Space Camp

MISSISSIPPI

Wikimedia Commons/Infrogmation

The Magnolia State

Capital – Jackson

State Bird – Mockingbird

State Tree – Magnolia

State Animal – White-tailed Deer

Largest City – Jackson

Smell the sweet magnolias. See the Old South mansions. Hear the slow Southern drawl. Mississippi charm! The state is bordered on the west by "Old Man River," the mighty Mississippi.

The weird-looking Portuguese man-of-war has a venomous sting! It lives near the surface of the ocean with its float below the water. While jelly-like, it is not a true jellyfish.

"Beautiful and scary at the same time."

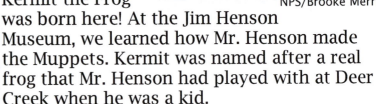

NPS/Brooke Merrill

Leland, MS: Kermit the Frog was born here! At the Jim Henson Museum, we learned how Mr. Henson made the Muppets. Kermit was named after a real frog that Mr. Henson had played with at Deer Creek when he was a kid.

John E. Barrett, courtesy of The Jim Henson Legacy Copyright2011-The Jim Henson Company Kermit the Frog copyright2011 The Muppets Studio, LLC

"Did you know that Oscar the Grouch was first orange? Mr. Henson made him green before the second season of 'Sesame Street.'"

Natchez, MS: At Mammy's Cupboard you eat in what looks like the skirt of a 28-foot bottle of Mrs. Buttersworth syrup. They have delicious sesame chicken salad on freshly baked sourdough bread, blueberry lemonade, chocolate pie....

"Mom loved the sweet tea and said the banana caramel pie was out of this world!"

flicker/livesimply

NPS

Natchez Trace Parkway: Bald cypress trees lose their needle-like leaves in the winter. They live best in areas that are flooded most of the time.

"We don't have cypress swamps like this in Maine."

Shrimp fishermen spread their nets out at sea. They know all about catching, cooking, and eating shrimp.

Mississippi Development Authority

Alexey Sergeev

The warm waters of the Gulf of Mexico wash up starfish and other animals on the beach. Star*fish* (sea stars) are not really fish. They are echinoderms like sand dollars and sea urchins. If starfish lose an arm, they can regrow one in about a year.

"Amazing! Wish people could do that."

LOUISIANA

Wikimedia Commons - public domain

The Pelican State

Capital – Baton Rouge

State Bird – Eastern Brown Pelican

State Tree – Bald Cypress

State Animal – Black Bear

Largest City – New Orleans

The Pelican State has tens of thousands of brown pelicans living along the coast. Pelicans build nests of grass that rise a foot above the ground.

Louisiana has parishes instead of counties. It also has the Superdome, Mardi Gras, and bayous.

Hurricane Katrina, which hit Louisiana in 2005, was one of the worst hurricanes in U.S. history.

Newellton, LA: These kids are having their picture taken with this 14-foot-tall mailbox. The mailbox measures 5 feet by 8 feet by 4 feet.

"I could lie down in it! I wanted to make a sign saying: HELP WANTED: TALL MAILMAN!"

Head to Toe Photos, LLC

New Orleans, LA: Louisiana is bordered by the Mississippi River on the east with its many swampy bayous (small, slow-moving rivers) feeding into the Mississippi. The Natchez steamboat, powered by a 26-ton paddle wheel, sails up and down the Mississippi near New Orleans.

"A lazy ride on the Mississippi."

New Orleans Steamboat Company

Wikimedia Commons/
Edd Prince

New Orleans, LA: Beads are thrown from parade floats as part of Mardi Gras. This huge party has been celebrated for over 150 years with parades, music, food, and costumes. Some people say that New Orleans is sinking because of all the Mardi Gras beads in attics all over the city.

"It looks like it rained beads!"

RedStickNow

Baton Rouge, LA: The old capitol of Louisiana, built in 1859, looks like a castle. It now houses the Museum for Political History and is also used for special events. The new 34-story capitol, built in 1932, towers over the city, making it the tallest capitol building in the U.S.

Barbara Pond

Spanish moss, abundant in the South, hangs from cypress trees in this swamp. Not true mosses, these air plants are related to the bromeliads, need no soil, and may slow the tree's growth by blocking light to its leaves.

NPS

"Jimmy says we need 'bearded' trees in our yard back home."

Taking a walk along the Creole Nature Trail can bring a few scary surprises. The Trail offers a good place to see hermit crabs on the beach. You might even see an alligator cutting across the path.

Cttagent

"Yikes. I wouldn't want one of those in my yard. But if we had a leash, we could 'walk' the dog... I mean alligator!"

byways.org – public domain

ARKANSAS

Shelba Oberto

- The Natural State
- Capital – Little Rock
- State Bird – Mockingbird
- State Tree – Pine
- State Animal – White-tailed Deer
- Largest City – Little Rock

Homework ideas are everywhere! We stopped at a Wal-Mart, and suddenly we had a research assignment. Did you know that Wal-Mart was started in Rogers, Arkansas, in 1962 by Sam Walton?

"I thought it was spelled Walmart!"

"Sometimes it is."

Many people come to "the land of opportunity" (the official state nickname prior to 1995) to see the rolling valleys and green mountains. Older folks here in the Ozarks sometimes still refer to those valleys and mountains as "hollers" and "knobs."

Eureka Springs, AR: Winding mountainside streets take you past Victorian houses and unique shops.

The five-story Christ of the Ozarks, the largest statue of Christ in North America, stands near the amphitheater of the Great Passion Play.

"It was neat seeing the statue from a distance surrounded by trees."

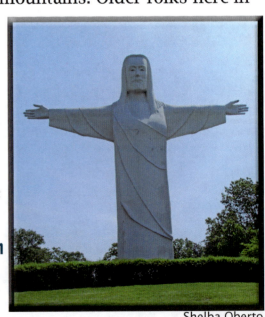

Shelba Oberto

≈ 52 ≈

The glass Thorncrown Chapel, which is made of 425 windows, rises up from this peaceful wooded setting.

Shelba Oberto

"The glass chapel would be a nice place for a wedding. Not that I'm getting married any time soon!"

AR Dept. of Parks and Tourism

Berryville, AR: Cosmic Caverns has two "bottomless" lakes, which means divers have never found the bottoms. What they *have* found are colorless trout and blind salamanders.

"It's creepy to think of a bottomless lake. Or a bottomless anything! But Mom gave us earth science homework today, so we are learning about these lakes."

davescove.com

"'Silent Splendor' is a room with 9-foot formations that look like straws."

Larry Campbell

Parthenon, AR: Beckham Creek Cave Haven, an awesome cave, has five bedrooms and baths, kitchen, great room, and a game room with a pool table, which became the guys' room.

"This was SO exciting! We got to spend a night out of the camper and not just in a regular motel! No kidding, it's a fancy cave!"

AR Dept. of Parks and Tourism

Murfreesboro, AR: These people are digging for diamonds at Crater of Diamonds State Park. Twenty thousand diamonds have been found since 1972.

"I wonder if they had any luck. This is the only place in the world where you can dig for diamonds, and it's finders-keepers!"

MIDWEST REGION

MISSOURI

Good news and bad news about Missouri: The good news is that we can thank the St. Louis World's Fair in 1904 for ice cream cones, though there is some disagreement about who actually invented them. Whoever it was, "take along" ice cream is a great idea!

The bad news is that New Madrid, in the southeastern corner of Missouri, was the center of our country's most powerful earthquake felt 1,000 miles away (1811-1812).

St. Louis, MO: The Gateway Arch is 630 feet tall—75 feet taller than the Washington Monument and twice as tall as the Statue of Liberty. Visitors can go all the way to the top and look out.

"In pictures it doesn't look very big, but it's huge in person!"

Haley Parker

The stainless steel Gateway Arch moves with the wind. Although usually swaying about a half inch, with winds of 150 miles per hour, it could sway up to 18 inches (9 inches each way). The foundation goes 60 feet into the ground.

"What a view from the top! You can see 30 miles in every direction."

Springfield, MO: Fantastic Caverns is America's only ride-through cave. We rode the red tram past stalagmites, stalactites, and soda straw formations. Just think: They were formed by water—one drop at a time!

Fantastic Caverns

"So much more fun than reading about it in science class!"

Clayton, MO:
The Brown Shoe Company has this giant sculpture – a shoe made of 2,000 aluminum shoes.

"We (girls) loved it!"

Branson, MO:
Branson has music shows, the Silver Dollar City theme park, and the world's largest Titanic model, which is half the size of the real Titanic. Our tickets had the names of real Titanic passengers. We touched an "iceberg" and walked the Grand Staircase.

Cheryl Verde

Dina Parker

"Now it's more to me than just a movie. It's a sad, true story."

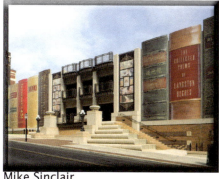
Mike Sinclair

Kansas City, MO: This Community Bookshelf—the front of the library's parking garage displaying 22 titles chosen by local residents—draws attention to the public library. Some of the children's books included are *Green Eggs and Ham, Winnie the Pooh, Little House on the Prairie, Goodnight Moon,* and *The Wonderful Wizard of Oz.*

≈ 55 ≈

IOWA

Shelba Oberto

Iowa, a leading farm state, is the only state bordered completely on the east and west by rivers (Mississippi, Missouri). Iowa's beautiful capitol has one gold dome and four copper domes.

The Hawkeye State

Capital – Des Moines

State Bird – Eastern Goldfinch

State Tree – Oak

State Animal – None

Largest City – Des Moines

dustin77A

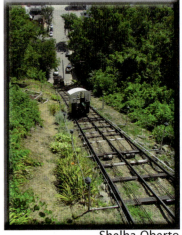
Shelba Oberto

Dubuque, IA: The Fenelon Place Elevator claims to be the world's shortest, steepest railway. Three states and the Mississippi River are visible from the top. It is a funicular railway meaning the two cars are attached by cable. One goes up, the other comes down.

"The cars pass halfway—really close!"

Iowa Tug Fest
Iowa Tug Fest

Le Claire, IA: Once a year, traffic on the Mississippi River stops for the Iowa vs. Illinois Tug Fest. A 2,400-foot, 680-pound rope is stretched between Le Clair, IA and Port Byron, IL. There are ten 20-member teams. Illinois is in the lead.

"I thought they were joking! But it really happens. A tug-of-war across the Mississippi!"

≈ 56 ≈

Shelba Oberto
Dina Parker

Pella, IA: Vermeer Mill is the tallest working Dutch windmill in the U.S. grinding wheat into flour. For the Tulip Festival in May, there are Dutch street washers, tulips, and wooden shoes everywhere. Pella set the Guinness World Record in 2010 for the most people dancing in wooden shoes—2,605!

"We found a picture of tulips in the snow!"

Amana, IA: The Amana Colonies are seven villages started by German immigrants. Visitors enjoy shops and good food—meats, cheeses, fudge, pastries, and more!

Shelba Oberto

Burlington, IA: Snake Alley was named the "Crookedest Street in the World" by Ripley's Believe It or Not. Lombard Street in San Francisco is another "crookedest" street.

"I could FLY down this on my bike if Dad would let me!"

"With these curves, CRASH would be more like it."

Urbandale, IA: Living History Farms—a popular interactive 500-acre outdoor museum—educates and entertains all ages. Visit three working farm sites: a 1700 Ioway Indian Farm, an 1850 Pioneer Farm, a 1900 Horse-powered Farm, and an exhibition center where visitors learn about 20th century farming. Stroll the streets of the 1875 town of Walnut Hill, where you can meet a blacksmith, explore the Print Shop and the General Store, and wander through Flynn Mansion and Church of the Land.

IA Tourism Office

"I couldn't believe how hard those farm families had to work just to eat."

Flickr/Picture Des Moines

ILLINOIS

Shelba Oberto

The Prairie State

Capital – Springfield

State Bird – Cardinal

State Tree – White Oak

State Animal – White-tailed Deer

Largest City – Chicago

Illinois trivia: The Chicago River is dyed green on St. Patrick's Day. Square dancing is the state dance of Illinois. Des Plaines, Illinois, was home to the first McDonald's.

Alton, IL: The tallest man in the world was Robert Wadlow. The "Gentle Giant" was an average baby, but by age 8, he was over six feet tall. When he died at age 22, he was almost nine feet tall and weighed 490 pounds.

"I felt really short next to Mr. Wadlow's towering statue."

Gene Kunz

The Metropolis Planet

Metropolis, IL: It's a bird! It's a plane! It's Superman! There really is a Metropolis, and it has lots of super stuff about Superman. The 15-foot statue dominates the middle of Superman Square. This 2008 photo shows the Guinness World Record being set for the most people dressed like Superman.

"I had my picture taken with Superman! So what if it's a statue?"

≈ 58 ≈

Skydeck Chicago

Chicago, IL: Days could be spent in the Shedd Aquarium and the Natural Museum of Science and Industry, but we wanted to see the Willis Tower, too. With 108 stories and 16,000 windows, the Willis Tower was, for many years, the tallest building in North America.

High speed elevators zip you up at 1,600 feet per minute.

"No stairs for us. We used the elevator."

The Ledge on the 103rd floor of the Willis Tower is for the fearless! Step out into a glass box that sticks out four feet and look straight down (about a half mile). Amazing! Then look all around. You can see up to 50 miles including four states.

"Fearless – that's me. But I almost wet my pants! Sorry, Mom!"

Skydeck Chicago

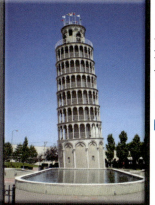
Wikimedia Commons – public domain

Niles, IL: The Leaning Tower of Niles, a replica of the Leaning Tower of Pisa in Italy, is only about half the size and half the leaning.

"Funny, but just standing and looking at it makes me want to lean."

Springfield, IL: President Lincoln moved from this 12-room home to the White House in 1861. Lincoln was the 16th president of the United States and led our country during the Civil War.

"He was shot at the Ford Theater, making him our first president to be assassinated."

NPS

INDIANA

Shelba Oberto

The Hoosier State

Capital – Indianapolis

State Bird – Cardinal

State Tree – Tulip Tree

State Animal – None

Largest City – Indianapolis

Indiana is the "Crossroads of America" because of all the interstate highways that come together in Indianapolis.

At the famous Indianapolis 500, race car drivers complete 200 laps. Fans pack the stands to watch their favorite driver compete for the checkered flag.

"Indiana produces a lot of popcorn—an important crop for our family's movie night!"

Elkhart County, IN: Over 20,000 Amish live in Indiana. They believe in simple clothes and a "plain" life—no electricity, telephones, or cars. Horse-drawn buggies and bicycles are everywhere. The Amish devote time to church and family. And, while they work hard, they still play and have fun just like us "Englishers."

"I had fun learning about the Amish!"

Shelba Oberto

David Leas

Greensburg, IN: Look closely at this out-of-the-ordinary courthouse. Tourists from about every state have come to see the trees growing on top!

"I wonder if they decorate it at Christmas."

IgoUgo.com

Indianapolis, IN: The Twisted House is not a real house but an art sculpture at Artspark. You can study and experience about 30 sculptures as you walk around this 12-acre outdoor art/nature park.

Wikimedia Commons/Chuck Carroll

Indianapolis, IN: To racing fans, the best thing about Indiana is the Indianapolis 500, a car race held each Memorial Day.

"Dad wishes we had planned our trip so we could have seen a race."

Turkey Run State Park: Sugar Creek is one of Indiana's most popular canoe streams. Sadly, because of pollution from farms and industry, no swimming is allowed in the creek.

"We decided to walk across Sugar Creek on the suspension bridge."

Wikimedia Commons/Daniel Schwen

OHIO

Shelba Oberto

The Buckeye State

Capital – Columbus

State Bird – Cardinal

State Tree – Buckeye

State Animal – White-tailed Deer

Largest City – Columbus

People who live in Ohio call themselves "Buckeyes" after their state tree. "Buckeyes" is also the name of the teams from Ohio State University. Ohio is renowned for its public library system, and Ohioans have always placed great value on education.

flickr/ronnie44052

The Rock and Roll Hall of Fame, here set against the Cleveland skyline, opened in 1995. There are four theaters and seven floors of exhibits telling the story of rock and roll music and performers.

"This was Mom: 'Oh, my goodness!'—'It's one of Elvis' cars!'—'Look at Michael Jackson's white gloves!' Geez, Mom!"

Sandusky, OH: Cedar Point claims to be the "Best Amusement Park in the World." There are 16 roller coasters, not to mention all the other rides and activities.

"My favorite is the Mantis—a stand-up roller coaster! WOW!"

Cedar Point

Newark, OH: This huge basket is not for picnicking. It is the 7-story office building of the Longaberger Basket Company and the world's largest basket.

"Mom loves her Longaberger baskets, but Dad and Jimmy weren't too excited."

Longaberger

Ohio Tourism Division

Pebbles, OH: Native Americans built the Serpent Mound about 1,000 years ago. An effigy mound is a raised pile of earth usually in the shape of an animal. These mounds had a religious purpose or were used as burial mounds. Serpent Mound, the largest ever found, is 1,300 feet (1/4 mile) long and three feet high.

"I wouldn't have had a clue what these mounds were if we hadn't done homework before we came!"

Holmes County, OH: The world's largest Amish community lives here. Their religious heritage—choosing to use buggies, farming with horses, and living "plain"—sets them apart from American culture. To respect their wishes, there are no front view photographs.

Holmes County Chamber of Commerce and Tourism

The Amish belief is based on the biblical text, "Do not love the world or things that are in the world. If anyone loves the world, love for the Father is not in him." 1 John 2:15 RSV

"Mom talked about how peaceful she felt in Amish country. I did, too."

OH Tourism Division

≈ 63 ≈

MICHIGAN

Shelba Oberto

The Wolverine State
Capital – Lansing
State Bird – Robin
State Tree – White Pine
State Animal – White-tailed Deer
Largest City – Detroit

Michigan is also called the Great Lakes State because it borders four of the five Great Lakes—Superior, Michigan, Huron and Erie. It has two parts, Upper Peninsula (U.P.) and Lower Peninsula. The above map shape includes both land and areas of the lakes that belong to Michigan.

Michigan has the only floating post office. The J. W. Westcott II delivers mail to the sailors that travel the Great Lakes.

Upper Peninsula: The U.P. has the Saulte Ste. Marie Canals (Soo Locks) which make it possible for ships to manage the 21-foot drop between Lake Superior and Lake Huron.

Detroit MI: Not only is the Detroit region the birthplace of the automotive industry, but more cars and trucks are produced here than in any other state in the country. In 2011, more than 1.9 million cars and trucks rolled off Michigan assembly lines, including over 1.5 million at assembly plants located in the Detroit region.

"We went to the Henry Ford Museum in Dearborn where we saw the first cars that were made and all kinds of experiments in cars since then."

Carscoops

Dina Parker

Dina Parker

Mackinac (pronounced Mackinaw) Bridge: The peninsulas are connected by the five-mile-long Mackinac Bridge (Mighty Mac). It is the longest suspension bridge in the Western Hemisphere.

"We saw large freighters and sailing yachts go underneath. It's pretty at night, too."

Mackinac Island, MI: The only way to get to the island is by small plane or ferry. Ferries go back and forth all day long, always passing by the Round Island Lighthouse.

Dina Parker

Dina Parker

The island's Grand Hotel has the world's longest porch—660 feet (longer than two football fields) with 260 flower boxes. You can rent horses, carriages, and bicycles. The island is eight miles around. No cars allowed! You can also tour Fort Mackinac.

"I loved the Victorian houses and shops. Jimmy liked the marina and fort. We all loved the fudge! We did not want to leave Mackinac Island!"

Grand Marais, MI: The Pickle Barrel House is only 16 feet tall, but there is a living room on the first floor, a bedroom upstairs, and a kitchen in a smaller attached barrel in the back.

"Mom says our homework is to find out what the 'Teenie Weenies' have to do with the Pickle Barrel House."

Grand Marais Historical Society

WISCONSIN

Dustin 77A

The Badger State

Capital – Madison

State Bird – Robin

State Tree – Sugar Maple

State Animal – Badger

Largest City – Milwaukee

The people of Wisconsin proudly claim the name "Cheesehead." The state is known for its great cheese.

The state boasts great natural beauty—it borders two of the Great Lakes and has 15,000 lakes spread throughout the state. The rocky cliffs of The Dells along the Wisconsin River attract tourists from all over the world. A bazillion waterparks add a lot of man-made fun!

Wisconsin River: The Dells Boat Tour took us by sandstone cliffs.

"We had a great view from the top level of the boat!"

Wisconsin Dells Visitors and Convention Bureau

The boat tour includes two stops. One is at Witches' Gulch where you walk on a wooden boardwalk through a slot canyon.

Dina Parker

Dina Parker

The other stop on the boat tour is at Stand Rock. We watched while a trained dog leaped from one rock bluff to another.

"Both stops were very interesting."

Madison, WI: It is summer—there's no ice—but this postcard about ice boating on Lake Mendota got my attention. Asking around, I learned that ice boats can go up to five times faster than the speed of wind. A wind of 20 miles per hour means speeds of up to 100 miles per hour!

TravelWisconsin.com

"Watch out on a windy day! There are no brakes!"

TravelWisconsin.com

Spring Green, WI: House on the Rock is impossible to describe. Each section has a different theme. Here are just a few. "The Streets of Yesterday" is an early American town. "The Heritage of the Sea" room has a 200-foot model of a whale-like creature. Then there is a room with a huge carousel and a large collection of automatic music machines called the "Music of Yesterday." The glass Infinity Room sticks out 218 feet and is 156 feet above the ground. There are 3,264 windows.

"I was scared walking out and looking down. We've never seen anything like this!"

Wisconsin Dells, WI: The Tommy Bartlett Thrill Show takes place on Lake Delton. This waterskiing and boat jumping show also features thrills on land. The man and woman in the photo are walking in spinning cylinders as the whole thing also spins.

"There's nothing boring about this show!"

Dina Parker

MINNESOTA

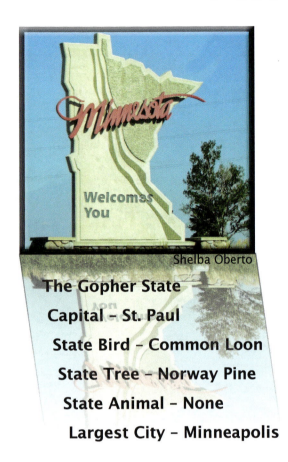
Shelba Oberto

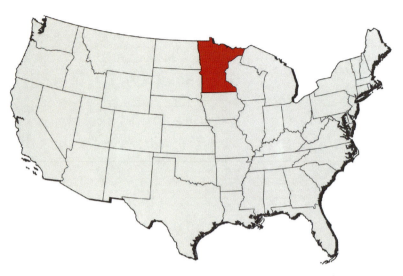

The Gopher State

Capital – St. Paul

State Bird – Common Loon

State Tree – Norway Pine

State Animal – None

Largest City – Minneapolis

Hello from Minnesota, Land of 10,000 Lakes! The Mississippi River starts as a small stream that we walked across in northern Minnesota.

The Mall of America, the largest mall in the U.S., is the size of 78 football fields and has an indoor theme park.

"Mom shopped 'til she dropped while Jimmy and I had fun at Nickelodeon Universe! Dad drank LOTS of coffee."

image191

Rochester MN: Home of the world-renowned Mayo Clinic. Founded by a father and his two sons, the Mayo Clinic, a not-for-profit institution, provides health care and health education for people who come from all around the world.

Blue Earth, MN: The Jolly Green Giant, symbol of the Green Giant food company, which is now a part of General Mills, is about five stories tall. A man on the platform would be about as tall as the giant's boots.

"He's huge and very green!"

Blue Earth Chamber of Commerce CVB

Split Rock Lighthouse: Over 100 years ago, this lighthouse was built along the coast of Lake Superior to warn ships of the rocky coast. Lighthouse keepers had to stay up all night, keeping the wicks trimmed, polishing the lenses, and keeping the mechanism working that turned the light.

MN Office of Tourism

rlukei

Eagles, who mate for life and like to return to the same nest, are making a comeback in Minnesota. This eagle couple is ready to create a family.

A bull moose, at home in the north woods, shows off his antler rack.

"Minnesota's lakes and forests are filled with wildlife."

byways.org – public domain

Red Wing, MN: The world's largest boot is 16 feet tall, 7 feet wide, 20 feet long, and would fit a 12-story giant! The Red Wing Shoe Company not only made this giant boot, but they make about 5,000 normal pairs of boots every day.

"The shoelace is 104 feet long!"

Jeff Marcus/Red Wing Shoe Company

Duluth, MN: While at Canal Park in Duluth, a busy port city on Lake Superior, we saw an ocean freighter come into port. Traffic on the Aerial Lift Bridge was stopped so the bridge could go up. It took about three minutes.

"We walked on the pier and waved at people on sailboats coming in from a day on the lake."

Shelba Oberto

NORTH DAKOTA

The Flickertail State

Capital – Bismarck

State Bird – Western Meadowlark

State Tree – American Elm

State Animal – Nokota Horse

Largest City – Fargo

North Dakota is nicknamed after all the flickertail ground squirrels that make their homes there.

North Dakota also has a state beverage – milk.

The Scheels store in Fargo is the world's largest all-sports store. It even has a Ferris wheel inside.

Fort Seward Wagon Train: In the old western movies, pioneers in the wagon trains circle their wagons at the end of the day, get grub from the chuck wagon, and sit around the campfire. Today, the Fort Seward Wagon Train ride takes a week traveling about 15 miles a day (3-4 mph).

"Someday I want to do this!"

Wikimedia Commons – public domain

Near Dunseith, ND: The International Peace Garden straddles the border. Two of the 120-foot concrete towers are in North Dakota, and two are in Manitoba, Canada. There is a Peace Chapel and 150,000 flowers.

Jamestown, ND: "Buffalo City" has the world's largest bison sculpture. The museum has three albino (white) buffalo. They are very rare (1 in 10 million) and sacred to Native Americans.

National Buffalo Museum/Felicia Sargeant

"The birth of a white buffalo calf symbolizes hope and a good future."

City Data.com

Oil was discovered in North Dakota in 1951. Since then, this state has become a leading exporter of oil. The oil boom has also given the state a billion dollar budget surplus.

Dunseith, ND: We are in the Turtle Mountains, and this is the W'eel Turtle made of over 2,000 steel tire rims. It is two stories high, and the head alone weighs over a ton.

"And the head moves!"

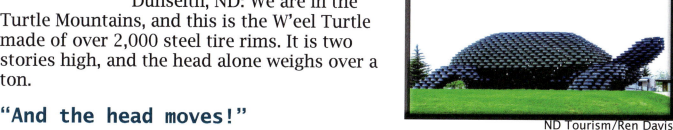
ND Tourism/Ren Davis

New Town, ND: North Dakota is full of Native American culture. One type of Native American home built in the Plains is the earth lodge with a smoke hole in the middle of the dome.

"Staying overnight in the Earth Lodge Village was really fun! One night out of the camper. Yes!"

ND Tourism/Heather LeMoine

SOUTH DAKOTA

SD Tourism/Chad Coppess

Mount Rushmore State

Capital – Pierre

State Bird – Ring-necked Pheasant

State Tree – Black Hills Spruce

State Animal – Coyote

Largest City – Sioux Falls

South Dakota is known for the Badlands, Black Hills, Corn Palace, Mount Rushmore, Wall Drug, Jewel Cave, Crazy Horse, and more.

Laura Ingalls Wilder, author of the *Little House* series, wrote about her life in South Dakota.

NPS

Hot Springs, SD: Wind Cave National Park, the first cave to become a national park, has the largest amount of boxwork (calcite in a rare honeycomb pattern) in the world. Mammoth Cave and Carlsbad Caverns are also national parks.

Notice Flat Stanley on the sign! Classrooms (usually 2nd-4th grades) all over the world read the *Flat Stanley* series and take part in the Flat Stanley Project.

"I did that project last year!"

Mitchell, SD: Every year the murals at the world's only Corn Palace are changed inside and outside, but a huge change is coming, including new lighted domes!

"I couldn't believe such interesting art was made from corn!"

Corn Palace/Mark Schilling

SD Dept. of Tourism

Iron Mountain Road has three tunnels and "Pigtail Bridges" that curve around like a curly pig's tail. Over a thousand buffalo roam freely in Custer State Park. When they cross the roads, everyone waits!

"Buffalo look clumsy, but they run fast!"

Near Rapid City, we squeezed our way up the Needles Highway with its needle-like granite formations. A tour bus barely made it through this tunnel.

"We all held our breath and then clapped when he made it."

Dina Parker

Keystone, SD: The entrance to Mount Rushmore has all the state flags. The presidents' heads are six stories tall and carved in granite. Gutzon Borglum carved the heads of Washington, Jefferson, Theodore Roosevelt, and Lincoln. They are lit up after dark.

"Way neater than the pictures!"

Dina Parker/Shelba Oberto

Black Hills: Crazy Horse is an enormous carving of a Sioux Indian chief. Construction began 65 years ago. When it is complete, it will be the largest mountain carving in the world. The inset photo shows what the completed sculpture will look like.

"Wow! They have a lot more to do before it's finished."

Dina Parker/Shelba Oberto

NEBRASKA

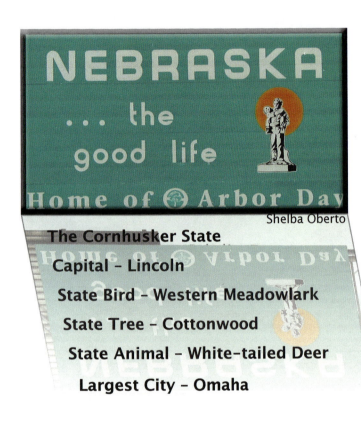

The Cornhusker State

Capital – Lincoln

State Bird – Western Meadowlark

State Tree – Cottonwood

State Animal – White-tailed Deer

Largest City – Omaha

Now we know why Nebraska is one of the Great Plains states. For miles and miles we traveled across flat grassland prairie.

But not at the Henry Doorly Zoo in Omaha! There you can wander through the world's largest indoor rainforest.

Ashland, NE: At the Strategic Air Command (SAC) Museum, visitors can climb inside aircraft like the B-52 bomber.

Gothenburg, NE: Barbed wire sculptures of a Native American on horseback and a buffalo bring a realistic feel to the Sod House Museum. Soddies, made of big chunks of sod carved out of the ground, had no air conditioning, no TV, no refrigerator, no toilet—well, there was an outhouse! We also saw a Pony Express station. In 1860-1861 the Pony Express delivered mail west of Missouri using relays of fast horseback riders. More than 100 stations were needed for riders to get fresh horses.

"Making barbed wire sculptures would be a prickly art. Well, at least tricky."

"No harder than living during that time in one of those sod houses."

Nebraska Division of Travel and Tourism/J. Nabb

Kearney, NE: The 309-foot Archway Monument is a two-story museum that goes back to the Old American West with exhibits like the Oxen and Covered Wagon Exhibit.

"This stretches all the way across the interstate. Can't miss it!"

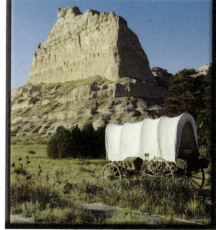
Nebraska Division of Travel and Tourism/R. Neibel

Scotts Bluff County, NE: Scotts Bluff National Monument juts up 800 feet right in the middle of the flat prairie. Over 100,000 visitors come every year to hike and climb.

Alliance, NE: England has Stonehenge, and Nebraska has Carhenge.

Nebraska Division of Travel and Tourism/D. Curran

These 38 cars were stacked up and painted gray during a family reunion. Weird!

"Never heard of the mysterious Stonehenge? Neither had I. But after seeing Carhenge, researching all about it became interesting homework!"

Hebron, NE: While sightseeing we got to swing in the world's largest porch swing. It holds 18 adults or 24 kids or 128 babies!

"I'm thinking—could be more or less depending on how skinny they are."

George Barker

KANSAS

Shelba Oberto

The Sunflower State
Capital – Topeka
State Bird – Western Meadowlark
State Tree – Cottonwood
State Animal – Buffalo
Largest City – Wichita

Kansas is the breadbasket of the country—a leader in growing wheat. It is also the second largest producer of beef cattle, behind Texas. Every type of prairie habitat is found here.

Pratt, Kansas, even has twin water towers that are labeled HOT and COLD!

Quinter, KS: Castle Rock looks out of place surrounded by flat prairie.

"But worth the bumpy road to it!"

Hutchinson, KS: The Kansas Underground Salt Museum covers 940 acres *underground*—650 feet below the ground. That is as far down as the Gateway Arch is up. About a half million tons of salt are mined out of here yearly which leaves empty space. Companies like Disney, Warner Brothers, and Sony have installed storage vaults to hold original films, costumes, and other important things. The tour is the only salt mine tour of its kind in North America.

Kansas Division of Travel and Tourism/ Barbara Shelton

"We had to wear hard hats and carry this breathing thing in case of an emergency. We got to keep a small chunk of salt."

Kansas Division of Travel and Tourism/Brian Lingle

Goodland, KS: The world's largest easel is about eight stories tall and weighs 45,000 pounds. It holds a huge copy (24 feet by 32 feet) of "The Sunflowers in a Vase" by Van Gogh. Artist Cameron Cross started the Van Gogh Project to put all seven of the famous artist's sunflower paintings in seven different countries. This is the third, after Canada and Australia.

"America's easel went to Kansas, which is the Sunflower State."

Cameron Cross

Liberal, KS: In *The Wizard of Oz*, Dorothy is swept away from Kansas by a tornado and tries to find her way home. The Land of Oz, here in Liberal, is a walk-through version of the movie. We saw a model of Dorothy's house, exhibits, and the Yellow Brick Road.

"*The Wizard of Oz* is one of my favorite movies! I like the Cowardly Lion, the Tin Man, and the Scarecrow."

Shelba Oberto

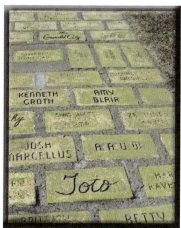
Shelba Oberto

Canton, KS: A buffalo calf stands close to her mother at the Maxwell Wildlife Refuge.

"In some parts of Kansas, buffalo are raised for meat. We ordered buffalo burgers for dinner one night."

Kansas Division of Travel and Tourism/Popular Photography

SOUTHWEST REGION
OKLAHOMA

The Sooner State

Capital – Oklahoma City

State Bird – Scissor-tailed Flycatcher

State Tree – Redbud

State Animal – Bison

Largest City – Oklahoma City

"Oklahoma has more Native Americans than any other state."

In the 1800s, five tribes were forced by the U.S. government to leave their homeland in the East and move into Oklahoma. The Cherokee Nation named this forced march "The Trail of Tears." Over 4,000 out of 15,000 Cherokees died during their journey. The other tribes were the Chickasaw, Choctaw, Seminole, and Creek.

Today, about two-thirds of the members of the Cherokee Nation live in Oklahoma, where they have their own government and businesses.

"We bought several of the baskets they wove."

Wikimedia Commons – public domain

Pops' Archive

Arcadia, OK: "I'm hungry!" wailed the kids from the back seat. The POPS Restaurant was worth their wait! They have food, fuel, and fizz. The world's largest pop bottle structure towers 66 feet in the air (more than six stories) and looks so cool—day and night!

"The big problem was trying to decide on a flavor! 500 flavors! I can't make up my mind when there are only five!"

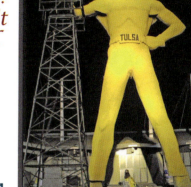
Wikimedia Commons/ Greg McKinney

Tulsa, OK: The Golden Driller, a symbol of the oil field workers, stands over seven stories tall and weighs 43,000 pounds. His right hand rests on an oil derrick.

"Its shoe size is 393 DDD! I wear a 3."

byways.org - public domain

Natural Falls State Park: Natural Falls, featured in the movie *Where the Red Fern Grows*, is so tall you could fit a seven-story building under it. The Cherokee call it "Dripping Springs."

"I read that book in school, and then saw the movie."

Millions of bison freely roamed the prairie before the settlers came. A bull bison like this one weighs about a ton (2,000 pounds) and measures six feet at the shoulders. Buffalo look slow, but they can outrun most horses.

Wikimedia Commons – public domain

"We took pictures from the safety of our car–thanks to our zoom lens."

byways.org - public domain

"Loved the stagecoach! It is so Wild West. But I can't imagine traveling for weeks and months in such a hot, bumpy, slow vehicle. I get restless in our air-conditioned car."

TEXAS

Shelba Oberto

The Lone Star State
Capital – Austin
State Bird – Mockingbird
State Tree – Pecan
State Animal – Longhorn
Largest City – Houston

The Johnson Space Center, NASA's Mission Control Center, is in Houston.

Texas has large ranches. The King Ranch is larger than Rhode Island.

The Sixth Floor Museum in Dallas, dedicated to the day President Kennedy was shot and killed there in 1963, captures that sad time in American history.

sanantonioriverwalk.com

San Antonio, TX: San Antonio is so interesting! The Riverwalk (Paseo del Rio) has shops, food, musicians, walkways along the San Antonio River (one level below the city), and river cruises.

"We spent a whole wonderful evening along the river, walking and taking the cruise."

San Antonio, TX: The battle cry, "Remember the Alamo," means more when you have actually been to the Alamo. Davy Crockett, who died in the Mexican attack on the Alamo in 1836, became one of the best-known American folk heroes.

"I once wrote about Davy Crockett for a history report."

San Antonio CVB

Dina Parker

San Antonio, TX: People of all ages learn from the exhibits at Sea World. This girl was having fun picking up the starfish (sea star) in the starfish pool and learning about the suckers underneath their arms that allow them to creep along the ocean floor. Starfish have no backbone and may range in size from a tiny centimeter to an awesome three feet.

"They push their stomach out through their mouth to eat! Yuck!"

Paris, TX: Paris, Texas, has a 65-foot-tall Eiffel Tower. Imagine 11 six-foot-tall men stacked on top of each other. A bit taller than the Texas Eiffel, the one in Paris, France, dominates the skyline at 986 feet!

Lamar County Chamber of Commerce

"Love the Texas cowboy hat on top!"

Bat Conservation International

Austin, TX: About one and a half MILLION bats fly out from under the Congress Avenue Bridge each night between March and November to look for food. This is the largest bat colony in North America.

"OK, bats are not my favorite, but this is bat-tastic!"

≈ 81 ≈

NEW MEXICO

Shelba Oberto

The Land of Enchantment

Capital – Santa Fe

State Bird – Roadrunner

State Tree – Piñon

State Animal – Black Bear

Largest City – Albuquerque

New Mexico, a land of contrast: canyons – mountains, forest – deserts.

Santa Fe is the highest capital city in the U.S. (about 7,000 feet).

Zuni, NM: Over 6,000 people live in the Zuni Pueblo, the largest of the 19 pueblos (Native American villages) in New Mexico. Zuni Mission, the historic church, has breathtaking murals depicting the spirits of the Kachina religion.

"Photography is not allowed in the church, so we are taking home a Kachina doll."

Las Cruces, NM: The world's largest roadrunner is a sculpture made of trash. Olin Calk created a 20-foot-tall and 42-foot-long "Big Bird."

"This 'Big Bird' isn't yellow."

"Real roadrunners like running (up to 15 mph) more than flying."

Myke Groves

Capitan, NM: In 1950 a little bear cub was found in a forest fire in the Capitan Mountains with burned paws. He became known as Smokey Bear and the symbol for fire prevention. He lived for 26 years at the National Zoo in Washington, DC. Now he is buried here at the Smokey Bear Historical Park.

Catella

"Forest fires kill more than trees. I feel sorry for the animals."

Carlsbad, NM: Carlsbad Caverns, one of the largest caves in the U.S., has over 110 rooms filled with stalactites and stalagmites.

"Since our spelunking day in Kentucky, we love caves."

NPS/Peter Jones

Ruidoso Downs, NM: The home of the Ruidoso Downs Racetrack is also home to the Hubbard Museum, a living museum which captures much of the life of the old west and features these sculpted wild horses.

Wikimedia Commons – public domain

Roswell, NM: Roswell has a UFO Museum because many people believe an unidentified flying object crashed near here in 1947.

"This McDonald's Play Place is like a flying saucer!"

Wikimedia Commons/AllenS - public domain

Albuquerque, NM: The Albuquerque International Balloon Fiesta in October is the world's largest hot air balloon festival. Over 100,000 spectators watch 600 balloons rise into the air.

"It would be awesome to be here during the festival."

Wikimedia Commons/NASA: Jay Levine – public domain

ARIZONA

Shelba Oberto

The Grand Canyon State

Capital – Phoenix

State Bird – Cactus Wren

State Tree – Palo Verde

State Animal – Ringtail

Largest City – Phoenix

Native American reservations make up about one-fourth of Arizona. Its desert is home to rattlesnakes, Gila monsters, and cacti.

The West's most famous gunfight, immortalized in the movie, "The Gunfight at O.K. Corral," took place in 1881 west of the O.K. Corral in Tombstone.

The Petrified Forest National Park is one of the largest and most colorful areas of petrified wood. These logs are really rocks. Law does not allow taking pieces from the park, but petrified wood found outside the park can be sold in shops.

"I bought a small piece to show in science class next year."

benkrut

Shelba Oberto

Fountain Hills, AZ: One of the world's tallest fountains has water shooting 300-560 feet high (ten feet higher than the Washington Monument). Near the fountain is Maytag Matilda. This horse is named after the Maytag washing machine that makes up part of her stomach. Dixie Jewett, an artist/welder, sculptured the horse out of recycled things…a coffee pot, license plate, iron, wheels…you name it!

Shelba Oberto

"There are so many different things. I tried to count but lost track."

Shelba Oberto

The desert is loaded with huge saguaro cacti. A 20-foot saguaro can weigh a ton and be 150-200 years old. We saw a cristate crown, something that forms in only 1 in 50,000 saguaro.

"That's kind of weird."

Amado, AZ: The Longhorn Grill grabs everyone's attention so they will stop to look and then eat. It is so—Arizonan!

Murray Bolesta

Grand Canyon: One of the Seven Wonders of the World, the Grand Canyon is so deep that from the top the rushing Colorado River looks like a trickling stream. The river slowly carved this gorge 277 miles long, a mile deep, and 4-18 miles wide.

"When I'm old enough, I want to ride a mule down into the canyon to look from the bottom up!"

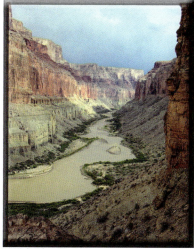
NPS/Mike Quinn

WEST REGION
NEVADA

pancaketom

The Silver State

Capital – Carson City

State Bird – Mountain Bluebird

State Tree – Single Leaf Piñon; Bristlecone Pine

State Animal – Desert Bighorn Sheep

Largest City – Las Vegas

Nevada, a dry, sagebrush-covered desert, is known as the gambling and entertainment capital of the United States (thanks to Las Vegas).

Las Vegas, NV: So this is Las Vegas! The huge hotels and casinos on the Las Vegas Strip come alive and dazzle with lights after dark. Gambling and shows entertain the adults.

"Thrill rides entertain the kids."

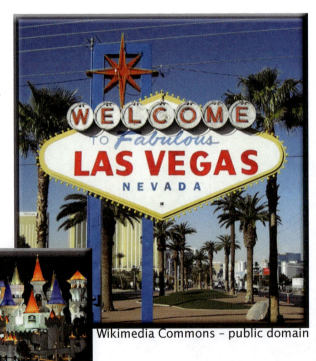
sainanirita

Wikimedia Commons – public domain

Las Vegas, NV: The Stratosphere: America's tallest free-standing observation tower. At the very top is "Insanity—the Ride"!

The ride moves up to 40 miles per hour and hangs 68 feet over the edge. All that at a height of 900 feet above the Las Vegas Strip!

Wikimedia Commons/Tim Jarrett   koby_dagan

"Kaylee and I were trying to decide if we wanted to try it. Then we saw the sign: Under age 15—Must ride with parent. That settled it. Mom and Dad weren't about to do a ride called 'Insanity'!"

"DO NOT TOUCH!" We have been seeing cacti everywhere, but only once did we see a bird's nest built in the cactus.

Shelba Oberto

While driving through barren land, we saw wild burros foraging for food. If left unchecked, the wild horse and burro population can double every four years. Thanks to the Adopt-a-Horse or Burro Program, each year many of them find adoptive homes.

kobby_dagan

Hoover Dam, one of the world's largest, is on the Colorado River at the Nevada-Arizona border. It formed Lake Mead, a huge reservoir. Everyone should take the Hoover Dam Hard Hat Tour. You learn things like: the dam is made from about seven million tons of concrete!

"So? They explained—that's enough concrete to pave a two-lane, 16-foot-wide and 8-inch-deep highway from San Francisco, California, to New York City."

Bureau of Reclamation

UTAH

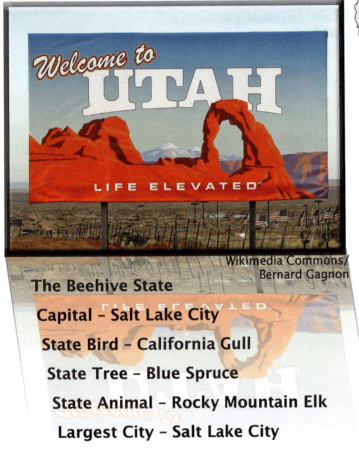

The Beehive State

Capital – Salt Lake City

State Bird – California Gull

State Tree – Blue Spruce

State Animal – Rocky Mountain Elk

Largest City – Salt Lake City

Why do people travel to Utah? They come to visit the five national parks, ski in the mountains, swim in the Great Salt Lake, see the salt on the Bonneville Salt Flats, and much more.

Beisea

The Great Salt Lake is the largest saltwater lake in the Western Hemisphere and much saltier than the ocean. Salt water is denser than fresh water, making floating easy. You will want to use the fresh water showers to rinse off the salt.

Salt Lake City, UT: The sound of the famous Mormon Tabernacle Choir fills the auditorium! 360 voices + an orchestra of 110 + an organ with 11,623 pipes = one fantastic sound!

"I'm sure they also practice a lot."

Wikimedia Commons – public domain

Monument Valley Navajo Tribal Park: These are called "The Mittens."

"That's easy to remember."

byways.org/A. E. Crane – public domain

NPS/Jonathan Parker

Zion National Park: Rainbow Bridge is the world's largest natural bridge. Don't miss a ride in the tour boat shown here entering Rainbow Bridge Canyon.

Then there is a slot canyon called "The Subway." Only serious hikers attempt this nine-mile hike.

NPS/Amy Gaiennie

"We need to come back to Zion and next time do the hike."

Bryce Canyon: Although not a true canyon, because it was carved by freeze-thaw cycles instead of a river, Bryce Canyon boasts many towers and spires. This photo shows "Thor's Hammer."

NPS/Ray Mathis

"I like Utah's national parks. We saw Zion, Bryce, Arches, and Canyonlands, but not Capitol Reef."

Bonneville Salt Flats: In this desolate area of Utah, a sculpture called "Metaphor, the Tree of Utah" rises up. Eight stories tall and made of 225 tons of concrete, its six balls are coated with natural rocks and minerals from Utah. The "tree" celebrates life in the midst of a desert.

Wikimedia Commons – public domain

"It seems odd that something made of concrete can celebrate life, but Mom says this tree symbolizes the joy of living."

COLORADO

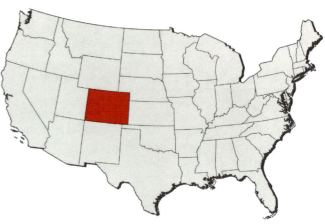

Shelba Oberto

The Centennial State

Capital – Denver

State Bird – Lark Bunting

State Tree – Colorado Blue Spruce

State Animal – Rocky Mountain Bighorn Sheep

Largest City – Denver

Colorado has 54 mountain peaks over 14,000 feet high.

The Royal Gorge Bridge is the highest suspension bridge in the world – 1,053 feet above the Arkansas River.

Denver, the "Mile High" capital, has the Denver Mint where coins are made. More than 50 million coins with the D mint mark can be made each day.

Rocky Mountain National Park: On Trail Ridge Road, you may find bighorn sheep, marmots, pikas, and herds of elk. A 300-pound ram may have horns that weigh 30 pounds, yet they still remain expert climbers.

NPS

Chryss Cada

The mountain slopes of Colorado attract skiers from all over the world. Gentle grades allow children to learn, but the steep craggy mountains challenge the best of skiers.

"I'm begging to come back here in the winter."

Cog Railway

Manitou Springs, CO: Katherine Lee Bates was awed by the view from Pikes Peak, which inspired her to write the words to "America the Beautiful." The Pikes Peak Cog Railway is an easy way to climb the 14,115 feet. Hard to believe that race cars actually race to the top of Pikes Peak every year.

Colorado Springs, CO: At the U.S. Air Force Academy, we saw cadets (students), airplanes, Falcon Stadium, and the Cadet Chapel which has 17 unusual spires.

Dina Parker

Dina Parker

Colorado Springs, CO: If your stomachs are on empty, you can refuel at the Airplane Restaurant—a Boeing KC-97 tanker—and learn about aviation history.

"I recommend the Air Tower Nachos and BBQ Bomber Burgers!"

Colorado Springs, CO: The Garden of the Gods has some odd rock formations like the "Kissing Camels" and "Balanced Rock."

"I'm wondering – when it topples, will it be called 'Unbalanced Rock'?"

Shelba Oberto

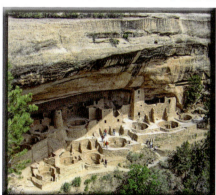
Rhett Farrior – public domain

Mesa Verde National Park: Take a look at the life of the Anasazi (ancestors of the Pueblo). Cliff Palace is the largest of about 600 cliff dwellings used for over 700 years. Cliff dwellers farmed by hand and hunted for food.

"I'm pretty sure they had no homework. Jimmy says that works for him!"

WYOMING

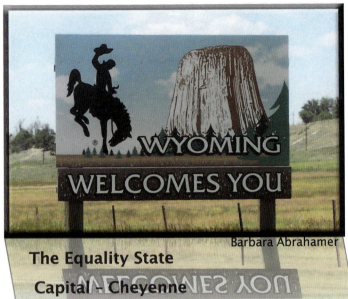
Barbara Abrahamer

The Equality State

Capital – Cheyenne

State Bird – Western Meadowlark

State Tree – Cottonwood

State Animal – Buffalo

Largest City – Cheyenne

Wyoming: Land of mountains, plains, sheep, cattle, oil, and mining. Fewer people live in Wyoming than in any other state.

It was the first state to let women vote, and Yellowstone Park, located mostly in northwestern Wyoming, was the nation's first national park.

Jackson, WY: Nestled in the Jackson Hole valley is Jackson, with its town square that attracts artists and tourists alike. At each of the four entrances to the town square is a large elk antler arch, made from antlers the elk have shed.

"For some reason elk shed their antlers every year. I wanted to go on an antler hunt!"

Wikimedia Commons – public domain

Just south of Yellowstone National Park and near Jackson is Grand Teton National Park filled with gorgeous jagged mountains.

NPS/Dave Smaldone

Yellowstone National Park: Tourists treasure the sights, the sounds, and the smells of Yellowstone! We watched Old Faithful Geyser, one of over 200 geysers, erupt. Steamboat Geyser is the world's largest active geyser. It erupts three times higher than Old Faithful, but Old Faithful is more famous because it erupts more regularly. Yellowstone is a geothermal area which means that the heat in the ground is near the surface.

NPS

"This place helps us understand all the activity that goes on under the ground we walk on, the ground that seems so firm."

Some of these mud pots smell like rotten eggs. They are like bubbling mud puddles with steam coming out of the ground. One trail was roped off because the ground was too hot to walk on.

"This may be geo...? Whatever, I still think it's spooky—listening to mud pots go, 'Blub, blub, blub.' Things here are very weird!"

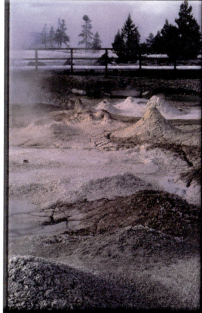
: NPS/Canter

Devils Tower, WY: Devils Tower, the first declared United States national monument, established in 1906, projects up 1,200 feet. The top is about the size of a football field.

"I can't imagine trying to climb those steep sides, but I guess people do. Some even make it to the top."

Wikimedia Commons – public domain

MONTANA

Wikimedia Commons/ Sebastian Bergmann

The Treasure State

Capital – Helena

State Bird – Western Meadowlark

State Tree – Ponderosa Pine

State Animal – Grizzly Bear

Largest City – Billings

We are in "Big Sky Country." Much of Montana is like being on the frontier. Some counties have only about six people per square mile.

At the Continental Divide, water flows to the Atlantic Ocean on one side and the Pacific Ocean on the other. At Triple Divide Peak, water also flows to the Arctic Ocean.

Glacier National Park: Scientists who study climate change are worried about glaciers all over the world. In this park there were 150 glaciers in 1850 and only 25 today. This climber on Lionhead Ridge appears to be on top of the world!

USDA Forest Service/Karl Birkeland

NPS

Depending on when you are there, breathtaking "Going-to-the-Sun Road" might have no snow or up to 80 feet of snow, which takes about two months to clear. This picture shows the road crew clearing the road in June!

"I wouldn't want their job!"

≈ 94 ≈

NPS

Glacier National Park: Mountain sheep, goats, pikas, elk, and marmots are some of the animals that live in the alpine tundra at high elevations. Goats walked right across the trail in front of us on Logan Pass.

Tourists enjoy stopping along the road to watch marmots. Or spot a grizzly bear.

"We saw lots of marmots, but it's probably a good thing we didn't see a grizzly."

Dina Parker

Utica, MT: Once a year ranchers make more than 50 hay sculptures for the Montana Bale Trail Festival (once called What the Hay Festival). Cars and buses from all over the West come to see the sculptures on the 21-mile stretch of highway.

"Cool idea!"

Mike Goad

Bozeman, MT: We knew nothing about ice climbing until now. In the winter, ice climbers scale the frozen waterfalls of Hyalite Canyon.

"One of the many things we have learned on this trip is how many dangerous activities people have turned into sport!"

Mike Harrelson

IDAHO

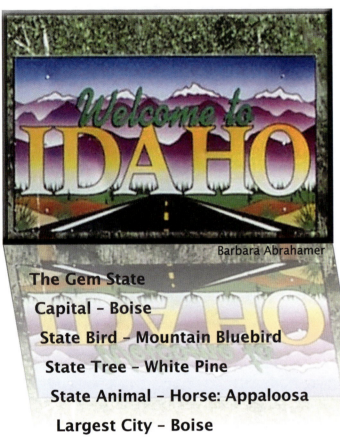
Barbara Abrahamer

The Gem State

Capital – Boise

State Bird – Mountain Bluebird

State Tree – White Pine

State Animal – Horse: Appaloosa

Largest City – Boise

Idaho got its nickname because it produces about 70 different gems used in jewelry.

Idaho grows most of our potatoes.

Hell's Canyon, the deepest gorge in North America, is over one and a half miles deep (8,043 feet), which is deeper than the Grand Canyon.

Due to dams and locks, Port of Lewiston is 465 miles from the Pacific Ocean, making it the farthest inland seaport on the West Coast of the continental U.S.

Cottonwood, ID: Since the camper seemed to be getting smaller, we were excited about getting a room at Dog Bark Park Inn bed and breakfast. What a fun place to stay! We slept in the nose of the world's largest beagle. The Sullivans, who are chainsaw artists, also carved Toby, a smaller 12-foot beagle and a fire hydrant outhouse.

"Dad said it was great being 'in the doghouse.'"

Dog Bark Park

Salmon, ID: Sacajawea, a Shoshone Indian, became the legendary interpreter for explorers Lewis and Clark. Sacajawea Heritage Days are celebrated here in Salmon, her birthplace. In her honor, the U.S. minted Sacajawea dollar coins in 2000.

"I have some of those dollars in my coin collection."

Idaho Tourism/Karen Ballard

Ketchum, ID: Trailing of the Sheep Festival honors the sheepherders' 100-year tradition of moving their flocks from summer mountain pastures to winter grazing in the desert. They parade the sheep right down Main Street.

Idaho Tourism/Carol Knothe

Shoshone Falls, known as the "Niagara Falls of the West," has spectacular falls that are actually higher than Niagara Falls in New York.

"I bet the first explorers were surprised!"

Idaho Tourism/Ron Gardner

Craters of the Moon National Monument and Preserve: Hot lava from volcanoes cooled and hardened into strange shapes named pahoehoe toes.

"Will there be homework on pahoehoe toes in our future?"

NPS

WASHINGTON

Jim Teresco

- The Evergreen State
- Capital – Olympia
- State Bird – Willow Goldfinch
- State Tree – Western Hemlock
- State Animal – Olympic Marmot
- Largest City – Seattle

Washington, the only state named after a president, prides itself on its apples, the Grand Coulee Dam, Boeing Company (airplanes), and the Hoh Rain Forest, which gets about 140 inches of rain each year. That's over 11 feet!

Five major volcanoes are part of the Cascade Range in Washington: Mount Baker, Glacier Peak, Mount Rainier, Mount Adams, and Mount St. Helens.

Mount St. Helens blew its top in 1980. The eruption killed 57 people, destroyed over 200 homes, and took 1,314 feet off the mountain top. The volcano rumbled and spewed again in 2004. Nature slowly restores the land.

"After learning about volcanoes, earthquakes, and geysers, I understand more about the constant underground shifting of the earth."

USGS/Austin Post – public domain

Yelp reviewer Sam S.

Spokane, WA: The world's largest concrete Radio Flyer wagon, measuring 12 feet high, 12 feet wide and 27 feet long, holds about 300 people.

"I had a blast climbing the steps at the back and sliding down the slide…uh, handle!"

Daniel Keebler

Mount Rainier: Majestic Mount Rainier, the tallest peak in the Cascade Range (14,410 feet or over two miles high), has not erupted for over 150 years, but is one of the largest and most dangerous volcanoes in the U.S.

"Schools near Mount Rainier have fire drills *and* volcano evacuation drills."

North Cascade National Park: Sure-footed mountain goats forage for food high in the rocky Cascades. This park used to have 318 glaciers, more than any other park in the continental U.S. Since 1980, all the glaciers have retreated and some have disappeared because of warmer weather.

NPS

City of Longview

Longview, WA: Squirrels crossing a busy street kept getting hit by cars so a 60-foot squirrel bridge was built over the street.

"This cute little bridge even gets decorated with lights at Christmas."

Seattle, WA: The Space Needle, with 848 stairs, an observation deck, and a revolving restaurant at the top, was built for the 1962 World's Fair. The elevator zooms up this 60-story structure in less than a minute. The Needle sways an inch for every 10 mile-per-hour wind.

"I'm glad we were here on a calm and clear day!"

Wikimedia Commons/Cacophony

ALASKA

Wikimedia Commons/ Richard Martin

The Last Frontier

Capital – Juneau

State Bird – Willow Ptarmigan

State Tree – Sitka Spruce

State Animal – Moose

Largest City – Anchorage

"Unreal! We just flew into Alaska, the largest state."

Vegetables can grow "super-size" because of summer days with about 20 hours of sunshine. Palmer, AK has grown softball-size radishes and 90-pound cabbages!

The four-foot-wide Trans-Alaska Pipeline carries oil 800 miles from Prudhoe Bay, America's largest oil field, to the port of Valdez. One of the world's most devastating environmental disasters caused by humans happened when a tanker spilled its oil into Prince William Sound in 1989.

The Iditarod Trail Sled Dog Race covers about 1,100 miles from Anchorage to Nome. The dog teams average 16 dogs, which means over 1,000 dogs leave Anchorage with their mushers.

NPS

Totem poles abound in Alaska due to the large Eskimo or American Indian populations. Because cities are so far apart, many families have a seaplane. In fact, you can only get to Juneau by boat or by plane.

"A family car with wings!"

Denali National Park: Mt. McKinley, the tallest mountain in North America, soars up over three and a half miles. From the air, it looks like a huge bump on the face of the earth.

"Flat Stanley has been here, too!"

"Looks like this brown bear will have tasty salmon for dinner."

These magnificent mountains receive a much-deserved standing ovation from this climber.

Our tour boat gave us an up-close look at this glacier, one of about 10,000 glaciers in Alaska. Known as calving, huge chunks of the glaciers are breaking off every year.

"These chunks become icebergs."

A spectacular display of aurora borealis or northern lights over Denali.

"Mom wants us to research what causes them."

Palmer, AK: We fed and petted real reindeer at the Reindeer Farm!

"Now back to Washington and our camper and on to Oregon, but please, can't we come back to Alaska again?"

Reindeer Farm

OREGON

- **The Beaver State**
- **Capital – Salem**
- **State Bird – Western Meadowlark**
- **State Tree – Douglas Fir**
- **State Animal – Beaver**
- **Largest City – Portland**

Oregon is known for lumber, Christmas trees, sea lion caves, and salmon fishing.

The Oregon flag has a beaver on the back making it the only state flag with different pictures on each side.

Cannon Beach, OR: While the Pacific Ocean was at low tide, we discovered tide pools filled with starfish, anemones, mussels, and sea urchins.

"This really excited kid on the beach had never seen tide pools before."

NPS

Wikimedia Commons/John Fowler

Haystack Rock, one of the largest monoliths or sea stacks on the Pacific coast, shelters tufted puffins nests on top. The rock is accessible on foot during low tide, but watch out for high tide to avoid swimming for shore.

"From a distance the rock seemed small, but when we got up close it was humongous!"

NPS

Crater Lake: This six-mile-wide volcanic crater holds the deepest lake in the U.S. The eruption of the cinder cone created Wizard Island. Some of the cliffs rise 2,000 feet above the lake. Take the 33-mile Rim Drive or hike down to the shore for a two-hour boat tour.

"The prettiest, bluest lake ever!"

Cape Meares National Wildlife Refuge: The base of the odd-shaped Octopus Tree spreads out 60 feet. Six candelabra-like arms on this Sitka spruce reach out 30 feet before turning up.

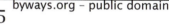
byways.org – public domain

Treehouses.com

Takilma, OR: We stayed at the Out'N'About Treesort! Sixteen different tree houses sleep 2-8 people each. We slept 35 feet off the ground in our Forestree.

"Awesome! Like a family camp. And out of the camper for two nights!"

Multnomah Falls on the Columbia River Gorge Scenic Highway: The water falls in two parts for a total of 620 feet. The footbridge above the lower falls makes a great photo spot. Unlike other famous waterfalls, Multnomah Falls does not dry up in late summer.

"Dad and Mom called this 'breathtaking.' I say, 'unbelievable,' 'absolutely beautiful,' 'gorgeous.' And Jimmy says, 'Way cool!'"

byways.org/Dennis Adams – public domain

CALIFORNIA

Barbara Abrahamer

The Golden State

Capital – Sacramento

State Bird – Valley Quail

State Tree – Redwood

State Animal – Grizzly Bear

Largest City – Los Angeles

While volcanic eruptions are not common in California (the last one on Lassen Peak in 1917), earthquakes are both common and feared. We toured the San Diego Zoo, Sea World, and Hollywood, where we walked on the stars on the Walk of Fame.

The California redwood trees are the tallest living things—taller than the Statue of Liberty—and one has a tunnel wide enough for a car to drive through. Imagine, a drive-through tree.

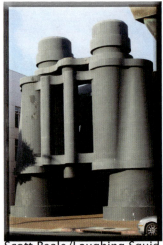

Venice, CA: Cars drive through the binoculars to enter the parking garage of this unusual binocular-shaped office building.

Scott Beale/Laughing Squid

"Mom calls it unusual. Kaylee calls it quirky. I say, 'What a fun place to work!'"

Death Valley Sand Dunes: Be sure to have plenty of water. Death Valley is the hottest, driest, and lowest place (282 feet below sea level) in the U.S.

"I bet that person wishes he had a dune buggy. Much more fun than walking!"

NPS

≈ 104 ≈

Anaheim, CA: The fantastic nighttime Electrical Parade, the Mickey Mouse sorcerer's hat, Cinderella's Castle.... Walt Disney knew how to make magic.

Dina Parker

"We loved a bazillion things! If only we could shorten the lines."

Wikimedia Commons/public domain

Los Angeles, CA: A tour of LA takes you from movie studios to movie stars' homes, from the J. Paul Getty Center to Knott's Berry Farm.

Dina Parker

"We would need a month to see everything there is to see."

San Francisco, CA: We were surprised that the Golden Gate Bridge is not gold but international orange. The bridge got its name because the water it crosses is the Golden Gate Strait.

Visitors thrill as their cable car hurtles down steep San Francisco streets.

Alcatraz Island in the background, once a federal prison known as "The Rock," is now a national park.

San Francisco CVB/Lewis Sommer
Wikimedia Commons /Cabe6403

NPS/Alexandra Picavet

Sequoia National Park: General Sherman, the largest tree (in volume) in the world, is over 2,000 years old and weighs as much as 360 elephants or 9 blue whales. Imagine a tree 274 feet tall (think of a 27-story building) and 209 feet around! It was named after Civil War General William T. Sherman.

"These are humongous! I remember my fourth-grade science teacher measuring 209 feet of rope so we could make a circle the size of General Sherman."

HAWAII

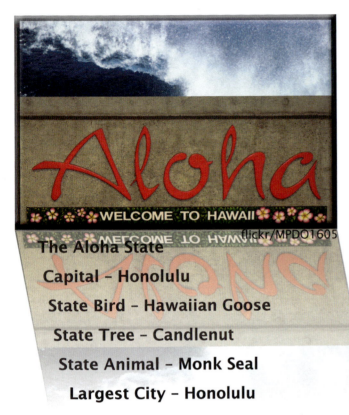

- The Aloha State
- Capital – Honolulu
- State Bird – Hawaiian Goose
- State Tree – Candlenut
- State Animal – Monk Seal
- Largest City – Honolulu

"Aloha from Hawaii!"

"No bridge to Hawaii. The car and camper are parked at the airport in California for a few days."

The Hawaiian Islands are actually a chain of eight main islands among a total of over 100. They are the tops of undersea shield volcanoes. The largest island is Hawaii, but the island of Oahu has the most people.

Important crops are sugar cane, pineapple, macadamia nuts, and coffee.

Many of the people are Japanese-Americans or Polynesians.

Japan attacked Pearl Harbor on Oahu in 1941, killing over 2,000 Americans and bringing the U.S. into World War II. Now this is more than just a topic in a history book. A song says, "Remember Pearl Harbor," and we will.

North Shore on Oahu: Catching the "big wave." Some say the world's best surfing is here.

"Awesome! I hold my breath when I watch them!"

Hawaii Tourism Authority/
Kirk Lee Aeder

Wahiawa, HI: The world's largest maze at the Dole Plantation (pineapple) is a-MAZ-ing. Most people make it through in 45-60 minutes. The record is about seven minutes!

"We are keeping our time a secret!"

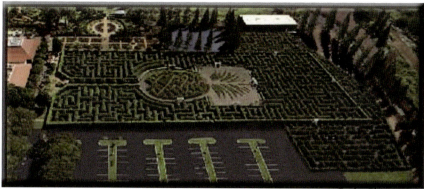
Dole Plantation

Hawaii Tourism Authority/Joe Solem

The hula is a graceful dance for all ages.

`"Kaylee took a hula lesson, but she needs help with her 'graceful' movements. I traded the hula lesson for a ukulele lesson."`

Island of Hawaii: The Holei Sea Arch is a natural stone arch here on the coast of the Big Island.

NPS

Hawaii Volcanoes National Park has REAL lava! The lava of Kilauea, the world's most active volcano, flows to the sea like a river.

Dave Boyle

"I will never forget seeing that lava. It made me more than a little nervous."

Our days of discovering the weird and wonderful places in the U.S.A. have come to an end. Hawaiians say we saved the best for last. But we must say "goodbye" to Hawaii and to all our travel adventures, fly back to California, and head for home. Thanks for coming along on our amazing ROADTRIP.

"ALOHA!"

`"ALOHA!"`

What Do You Remember About the Northeast Region?

1. What is an estuary?
2. What building in New York City towers over the 9/11 memorial reflecting pools?
3. Why is Atlantic City, New Jersey, called "Monopoly City"?
4. Most of the lobsters we eat come from which state?
5. Which state is the smallest?
6. What state capital is the smallest?
7. How many states are in New England?
8. In what year were the 9/11 terrorist attacks?
9. What was the first state?
10. Why is Ellis Island, New Jersey, important?
11. Where is the Monster Monument?
12. How long is the Boston Marathon?
13. How is the gondola powered?
14. How wide is the Skinny House in Boston?
15. Which state leads in maple syrup production?
16. What is "Eartha"?
17. How many spikes are in the Statue of Liberty crown?
18. What does Queen Connie in Vermont hold in her hand?
19. What is the highest mountain in the Northeast?
20. What supposedly happens if Punxsutawney Phil sees his shadow on February 2?
21. Where is the "sweetest place" on Earth?
22. What is odd about the Gillette Castle in Connecticut?
23. Who is the "Father of American Literature"?
24. What is unusual about Mt. Washington in New Hampshire?
25. Where do wild horses roam freely on the beach?

Dover Motorsports, Inc.

Maryland Office of Tourism

Answers on page 118

Fun Activities for the Northeast Region!

1. Construct a lighthouse with these materials: 18 oz. plastic cup for the base, 9 oz. clear plastic cup for the top, battery-operated tea light for a beacon, paper and markers to decorate the base, and a small piece of clear tape to join the base and top. Carefully lifting one side of the top will allow access to the tea light.

2. Print or trace an outline map of the U.S. and label the eleven Northeast states. Use a green colored pencil to lightly color the Northeast Region.

3. Acadia National Park is the only national park in the Northeast Region. Name the state it is in and at least five other facts about the park.

4. Visit a nearby cemetery and search for old gravestones. Make a tombstone rubbing. Use an old relative's grave, if possible.

flickr/Doug Kerr

5. Write a report about maple syrup production titled: "From Sap to Syrup."

6. Explain how leaves change colors, and write a poem about the beautiful fall colors in the Northeast.

7. Scrimshaw is the art of carving pictures in bone or ivory and was often done by sailors on whaling ships. Research the topic: scrimshaw for kids. Create a design and make a scrimshaw piece from a bar of Ivory soap.

8. Read *If You Give a Moose a Muffin* (ages 4-8, but all ages love the pictures!).

9. Time a one-mile walk/run with an adult. How much time would a 26-mile marathon take?

10. Write a humorous story about a blue lobster and tell about lobster fishing.

11. Make a simple kaleidoscope. Using a clear plastic sheet (like a report cover), draw a 4-inch by 8-inch rectangle. Cut out the rectangle and fold into three equal pieces (1¼ inches each). Fold up the ¼ inch and tape it on the outside with clear tape. Slide this inside a paper towel tube. Cover one end with a black construction paper circle with a hole in the middle to look through. On the other end, place a 4-inch square of plastic wrap. Push it in slightly to make a pouch in which you place tiny glass beads of various colors. Cover with another layer of plastic wrap. Secure with a rubber band or tape. Trim the plastic wrap to make it neater and decorate the tube with stickers, markers, or wrapping paper. Point your new kaleidoscope toward a light and enjoy!

12. Can your ancestry be traced back to Ellis Island? Make a family tree (free forms are available on the Internet).

13. Learn about the eight flags used at a NASCAR race. Find out the meaning of these flags: green, yellow, red, black, black with a white X, blue with a yellow stripe, white, and checkered.

14. Make a cake in the shape of one of the Northeast states.

15. Make a castle diorama.

16. Read *Misty of Chincoteague* (ages 8 and up).

17. Design a new flag for one of the Northeast states.

18. Write a recipe for "New England Flatcakes." Hint: Ingredients include blueberries and maple syrup for topping. Prepare and enjoy!

Bigstock/Kingjon

What Do You Remember About the Southeast Region?

Bob Balmut

1. What city is the country music capital?
2. When do sea turtles hatch?
3. What is the most visited national park?
4. In which state was Kermit the Frog born?
5. Where can you dig for diamonds and keep what you find?
6. Where is the largest statue of Christ in North America?
7. Where is the world's largest baseball bat?
8. What is the longest cave system in the world, and which state is it in?
9. How many presidents are featured in Presidents Park?
10. What are the first and second most visited homes in the U.S.?
11. What is the oldest city in the U.S., and in which state is it?
12. Who was Anne Sullivan?
13. In what state did the Civil War begin?
14. Which state has the tallest capitol building?
15. What is spelunking?
16. Which theme park is the most visited?
17. What is the largest house in the U.S.?
18. What is a starfish?
19. Where is America's tallest lighthouse?

Travel Berkeley Springs/Steve Shaluta-public domain

20. Where is the world's largest museum about space?
21. What state has swamps, alligators, Spanish moss and was hit by Hurricane Katrina?
22. The "smiling peanut" honors which president?
23. Where is the world's largest aquarium?
24. What is the Pentagon?
25. What event is held at the New River Gorge Bridge?

NPS

Answers on page 118

≈ 110 ≈

Fun Activities for the Southeast Region!

1. On your U.S. outline map, label the twelve Southeast states, and use an orange colored pencil to lightly color the Southeast Region.
2. Report on one of the following: spelunking (including information about stalactites, stalagmites, soda straws, and cave pearls) or airplane flight (including explanations of drag, lift, thrust, and gravity).
3. Georgia is known for peaches. Find a recipe using peaches, make (with adult supervision), and enjoy!
4. The Civil War began in South Carolina. Name the two sides in the war and tell why the war was fought.
5. There are nine national parks in the Southeast Region. Choose the one you think would be your favorite and tell why. Write a report about that national park.
6. List all 43 presidents in the order that they were in office. Build a castle with LEGOS.

CarlineB

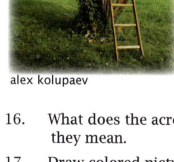
alex kolupaev

7. Write an acrostic using the letters in HOMEWORK.
8. Build a pentagon out of toothpicks.
9. Tell about the Underground Railroad and Harriet Tubman.
10. Tobacco is grown in the Southeast. Tell how tobacco is harmful.
11. Explain how loggerhead turtle hatchlings are being protected.
12. A pentagon is a five-sided figure. What are three-sided, four-sided, six-sided, seven-sided, and eight-sided figures called?
13. Read the book *Swiss Family Robinson* (ages 9+). A Stepping Stone version is also available for ages 6-9.
14. Are there tree houses where you live? Draw a picture of a tree house that you would like to build.
15. Draw and color a picture of what your favorite Cabbage Patch Kid would look like.
16. What does the acronym, NASA, stand for? Make a list of five or more acronyms and what they mean.
17. Draw colored pictures to illustrate the differences between the original Mickey Mouse and Mickey Mouse today, and write a poem using at least five Disney characters.
18. Name the four Southeast states that were part of the original thirteen colonies.

Original Appalachian Artworks

What Do You Remember About the Midwest Region?

1. Where is the world's largest Amish community?
2. What island has the Grand Hotel and no cars?
3. What is the W'eel Turtle made of?
4. What is Carhenge?
5. What famous building in Chicago, Illinois, has 108 stories, including the "Ledge"?
6. What is America's only ride-through cave?
7. Where is the "Land of 10,000 Lakes"?
8. What is the Jolly Green Giant?

monkeybusiness images

Dina Parker

9. Where is the only Corn Palace, and why is it unique?
10. In which state is House on the Rock?
11. Where is the world's largest Titanic model?
12. What is Snake Alley?
13. Which state leads in the production of cars and trucks?
14. What does the Mackinac Bridge connect?
15. What is the name of the world-famous medical center located in Minnesota?
16. Who are the four presidents carved on Mount Rushmore?
17. What stainless steel monument is twice as tall as the Statue of Liberty? Where is it?
18. Where is the world's largest easel? A copy of what painting is on display?
19. Ice boats can go how much faster than the speed of the wind?
20. Which two states have a tug-of-war across the Mississippi River?
21. What group of people lives the "plain" life?
22. Who made Effigy Mounds?
23. Where is the International Peace Garden?
24. Duluth, Minnesota, is a busy port on which Great Lake?
25. How is the space at the Kansas Underground Salt Museum used?

gubh83

Answers on page 118

Fun Activities for the Midwest Region!

1. Read the *Wonderful Wizard of Oz* (ages 8+) and draw your favorite character.

2. Tornadoes are common in the Midwest. Do tornadoes and hurricanes occur where you live? Make a chart comparing and contrasting tornadoes and hurricanes. What preparations could protect your family from each type of storm?

3. Choose to make a report about the Titanic or about albino animals. Better yet, do both!

4. The Indy 500 is 500 miles long. Find out the length of the track, how many laps make a race, how many cars can race, and what speeds they normally reach. Racing enthusiasts – design a race car!

WikimediaCommons/ Llamabr

5. The Midwest Region can be divided into two groups: Great Lakes states and Plains states. List the states in each group.

6. Research and write about Mackinac Island's three-mile "ice bridge."

7. Choose one Midwest state and design a new state license plate.

8. Describe the Effigy Mounds in Iowa.

9. The Midwest grows a lot of wheat. Make a whole wheat snack. Enjoy!

10. Write a haiku about something of interest in the Midwest Region.

11. Write a story about what life would be like as an Amish boy or girl.

12. Cars are produced along an assembly line. Plan a simple project that could be made using an assembly line.

Shelba Oberto

13. Mount Rushmore has stone carvings of the heads of four presidents. Give the reason each one may have been chosen. If you were carving Mount Rushmore today, which four presidents would you choose and why? You may change some or all of the presidents.

14. Using your U.S. outline map, label the twelve Midwest states and the five Great Lakes. Lightly color the Midwest Region with a blue colored pencil.

15. Read the history of the Pickle Barrel House and the Teenie Weenies. Make your own cartoon strip starring the Teenie Weenies.

16. Read about the Leaning Tower of Pisa in Italy to learn why it leans.

17. The bald eagle is the U.S. national bird. Draw a picture of a bald eagle and list some facts about it: size, color, habitat, mating, the number of eggs they usually lay, size of nest, and so on.

18. Read *Flat Stanley* books (ages 6-10). If your school is not involved with the Flat Stanley Project, you can do it from home. A free Flat Stanley app is also available through iTunes.

Eagle

What Do You Remember About the Southwest Region?

1. Where is the largest hot air balloon event held?
2. How do starfish move along the ocean floor?
3. What are the two things to see in Fountain Hills, Arizona?
4. What is the world's largest roadrunner made of?
5. How fast can roadrunners run?
6. What was the "Trail of Tears"?
7. What river carved out the Grand Canyon?
8. Which are faster – horses or buffalo?
9. Where is the Petrified Forest National Park?
10. Which president was killed in Dallas, Texas, in 1963?
11. Where is the largest bat colony in North America?
12. Why does Roswell, New Mexico, have a McDonald's Play Place resembling a flying saucer?
13. What restaurant has the world's largest pop bottle, and what state is it in?
14. Which state has more Native Americans than any other state?
15. Where did Smokey Bear live most of his life?
16. How much of Arizona is made up of Native American reservations?
17. In which state do most of the members of the Cherokee Nation live?
18. Where is the highest capital city in the U.S.?
19. Where is the Riverwalk (Paseo del Rio)?
20. What structure can Paris, Texas, boast about having?
21. How many states are in the Southwest Region?
22. How rare is a saguaro cactus with a cristate crown?
23. Natural Falls appeared in what movie?
24. What American folk hero died at the Alamo?
25. The rooms of Carlsbad Caverns have an abundance of what natural features?

Myke Groves

Ilike

Steve Oberto

Answers on page 118

Fun Activities for the Southwest Region!

1. The Southwest Region has a strong Native American culture. Make a paper placemat decorated with a Navajo design.

2. Make an illustrated report about the different Native American homes of the Southwest and the tribes that lived in each.

3. People (age 10+) can pay to ride a mule down into the Grand Canyon. Tell what you think you would like and dislike about such an adventure.

4. Read about the world's smallest museum in Superior, Arizona, and tell about the legend of the Apache Tears stone.

New Mexico Tourism Dept./ Mike Stauffer

5. Plan a trip to the Southwest state of your choice. Check out that state's tourism website, and name all the places you would want to see during your visit.

6. Draw, color, and label six different cacti from the deserts of the Southwest.

7. James Bowie and David Crockett were famous Texas cowboys. Write a paragraph about what happened to them and where.

8. Draw the French Eiffel Tower and the Texas Eiffel Tower to scale which will show the difference in heights. Remember the Texas cowboy hat!

9. Report on one or more of these desert animals: rattlesnake, tarantula, scorpion, coyote, bobcat, javelin, Gila monster, and horned toad.

10. Draw a desert picture showing all of the animals above.

11. Learn about the Roswell UFO incident. Let your imagination soar and write an exciting illustrated UFO story!

12. On your U.S. outline map, label the four Southwest states. Using a yellow colored pencil, color the states in the Southwest Region.

13. Cut a large bat out of black construction paper and a slightly smaller bat out of white paper. Tape the white paper to the back of the black bat. On the paper, write five to ten facts about bats.

14. Read *Rápido, the Roadrunner* available in digital format.

15. Write a poem about the desert.

16. Make a roadrunner cartoon strip.

17. Research the Chisholm Trail.

18. Explain how wood becomes petrified.

19. Read *Where the Red Fern Grows* (ages 8 and up).

20. Tell what a dude ranch is and what activities you would do there.

Anton Foltin

What Do You Remember About the West Region?

1. What is the hottest, driest, lowest place in the U.S.?
2. What large dam in on the Nevada-Arizona border?
3. What mountain erupted in Washington in 1980?
4. What do you expect to see at Mesa Verde National Park?
5. What is the "Niagara of the West"?
6. Which national park is a geothermal area? What is a geothermal area?

Marmion

7. What is often the "family car" in Alaska?
8. Which state is made up of volcanic islands?
9. What national park has the world's largest tree?
10. Which is saltier, the ocean or the Great Salt Lake?
11. The view from Pikes Peak inspired what song?
12. Where is Going-to-the-Sun Road?
13. Why is Bryce Canyon in Utah not a true canyon?
14. Where is the "Happiest Place on Earth"?
15. Which state has a bridge for squirrels?

Dina Parker

16. Which geyser in Yellowstone National Park is the most well-known? Is the largest?
17. Where is Kilauea, the world's most active volcano?
18. What is unusual about the Dog Bark Park Inn in Idaho?
19. What is the deepest lake in the U.S.? And where is it?
20. What city and state has "Insanity – the Ride"?
21. What are the tallest living things?
22. What is it called when pieces of glaciers break off?
23. What do you stay in at the Treesort in Oregon?
24. What is the "Mile High" capital?
25. What is the Continental Divide?

Andy Dean Photography

Answers on page 118

FUN ACTIVITIES FOR THE WEST REGION!

1. With a pencil, draw the ground and a large saguaro cactus on stiff white paper. Mix some salt with tan tempera paint and paint the ground. Mix salt with green tempera paint to paint the cactus. Let the picture dry completely.
2. Make a facts chart for Alaska and Hawaii. Include the year each became a state, the size and type of population, land size, landforms, and any other information you can find.
3. The West Region can be divided into two groups: the Mountain states and the Pacific states. List the states in each group.
4. Choose one of the following animals: marmot, pika, mountain sheep, elk, moose, or mountain goat. Write a short report about the animal including a picture.
5. Make a lei using construction paper or tissue paper, straws, and yarn or string.
6. Make a volcano and do a vinegar and baking soda eruption.
7. Write a report about the life of Walt Disney.
8. On your U.S. outline map, label the eleven states in the West. Using a red colored pencil, lightly color the West Region.
9. Write a report about the Anasazi cliff dwellers.
10. Write an acrostic using the letters in: MICKEY MOUSE.
11. Write a humorous story about a boy or a girl and a pet burro.

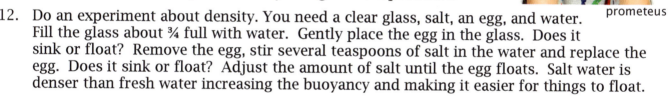
prometeus

12. Do an experiment about density. You need a clear glass, salt, an egg, and water. Fill the glass about ¾ full with water. Gently place the egg in the glass. Does it sink or float? Remove the egg, stir several teaspoons of salt in the water and replace the egg. Does it sink or float? Adjust the amount of salt until the egg floats. Salt water is denser than fresh water increasing the buoyancy and making it easier for things to float.
13. The Pikes Peak International Hill Climb (hill???) is awesome! Find out how long the course is, how many turns there are, and what the elevation is at the start and finish. What is the record time for this "Race to the Clouds"?
14. Make a "Northern Lights" painting using watercolor paints.
15. The world's largest maze in Hawaii would be fun, but for those of us not in Hawaii, we can find free mazes on the computer. Go to: krazydad.com/mazes
16. Do some research about the movements in hula dancing and perform for your parents or friends.
17. Write a report about Death Valley.
18. Tell something about each of the national parks in Utah.
19. Choose one of the state names and write an acrostic poem.

Mrs. Oberto, the author of this book, would like to hear about your experiences taking this *Roadtrip*. What was most interesting? What would be your favorite places to visit?

Email her at: obertobooks@gmail.com

Hawaii Tourism Authority

Answers

Northeast Region
1. Where fresh river water mixes with salty ocean water
2. One World Trade Center
3. Atlantic City street names and places are used on the Monopoly game board.
4. Maine
5. Rhode Island
6. Montpelier, Vermont
7. Six states
8. 2001
9. Delaware
10. About 12 million immigrants entered the U.S. through Ellis Island.
11. Dover International Speedway in Delaware
12. Twenty-six miles
13. The gondolier uses a 14-foot oar.
14. Ten feet
15. Vermont
16. The world's largest rotating glass globe
17. Seven
18. Full-sized VW car
19. Mt. Washington
20. There will be six more weeks of winter.
21. Hershey, Pennsylvania
22. None of the 47 doors are alike
23. Mark Twain (Samuel Clemens)
24. Its record wind speed of 231 mph
25. Assateague Island, Maryland

Southeast Region
1. Nashville, Tennessee
2. At night
3. Great Smoky Mountains National Park
4. Mississippi
5. Crater of Diamonds State Park in Arkansas
6. Eureka Springs, Arkansas
7. Louisville, Kentucky
8. Mammoth Cave National Park in Kentucky
9. 43
10. First—The White House, Second—Graceland
11. St. Augustine, Florida
12. Helen Keller's teacher
13. South Carolina
14. Louisiana
15. Cave exploring
16. Walt Disney World
17. Biltmore House
18. An echinoderm
19. Cape Hatteras, North Carolina
20. Huntsville, Alabama
21. Louisiana
22. Jimmy Carter
23. Atlanta, Georgia
24. U.S. military headquarters
25. Bridge Day for parachuters and rappellers

Midwest Region
1. Ohio
2. Mackinac Island
3. 2,000 tire rims
4. A display of 38 cars painted gray and stacked in an odd formation
5. The Willis Tower
6. Fantastic Caverns
7. Minnesota
8. The symbol of the Green Giant food company
9. Mitchell, South Dakota. The murals are made of corn.
10. Wisconsin
11. Branson, Missouri
12. Crookedest street in the world
13. Michigan
14. The Upper Peninsula and Lower Peninsula of Michigan
15. Mayo Clinic
16. Washington, Jefferson, Theodore Roosevelt, and Lincoln
17. The Gateway Arch in St. Louis, Missouri
18. Kansas. "Sunflowers in a Vase" by Van Gogh
19. Five times faster
20. Iowa and Illinois
21. Amish
22. Native Americans
23. Between North Dakota and Manitoba, Canada
24. Lake Superior
25. Companies have storage vaults there.

Southwest Region
1. Albuquerque, New Mexico
2. There are suckers underneath their arms.
3. Maytag Matilda and one of the world's tallest fountains
4. Trash
5. Up to 15 mph
6. In the 1800s, five Native American tribes in the east were forced to move to Oklahoma. The Cherokee Nation named their forced relocation "The Trail of Tears."
7. Colorado River
8. Buffalo
9. Arizona
10. President Kennedy
11. Austin, Texas
12. Many people believe a UFO crashed near there in 1947.
13. POPS Restaurant in Oklahoma
14. Oklahoma
15. National Zoo in Washington, DC
16. One-fourth
17. Oklahoma
18. Santa Fe, New Mexico
19. San Antonio, Texas
20. An Eiffel Tower
21. Four
22. One in 50,000
23. *Where the Red Fern Grows*
24. Davy Crockett
25. Stalactites and stalagmites

West Region
1. Death Valley in California
2. Hoover Dam
3. Mount St. Helens
4. Cliff dwellings
5. Shoshone Falls
6. Yellowstone—an area where the heat in the ground is near the surface.
7. A seaplane
8. Hawaii
9. Sequoia National Park
10. Great Salt Lake
11. "America the Beautiful"
12. Glacier National Park in Montana
13. It was carved by freeze/thaw cycles, not a river.
14. Disneyland in Anaheim, California
15. Washington
16. Old Faithful; Steamboat Geyser
17. Hawaii
18. Guests sleep in the world's largest beagle dog.
19. Crater Lake in Oregon
20. Las Vegas, Nevada
21. California redwood trees
22. Calving
23. Tree houses
24. Denver, Colorado
25. Where water on one side flows to the Atlantic Ocean and water on the other side flows to the Pacific Ocean.

Made in the USA
Charleston, SC
22 November 2015